THE BERRIGANS

GARLAND REFERENCE LIBRARY
OF THE HUMANITIES
(VOL. 154)

THE BERRIGANS
A Bibliography of Published Works by Daniel, Philip, and Elizabeth McAlister Berrigan

Anne Klejment

GARLAND PUBLISHING, INC. • NEW YORK & LONDON
1979

Library of Congress Cataloging in Publication Data

Klejment, Anne.
   The Berrigans.

   (Garland reference library of the humanities ; v. 154)
   Includes indexes.
   1. Berrigan, Daniel—Bibliography.   2. Berrigan,
Philip—Bibliography.   3. Berrigan, Elizabeth
McAlister—Bibliography.   I. Title.
Z8091.42.K55   [BX4705.B38]   016.3224′4   78-68214
ISBN 0-8240-9788-2

Printed on acid-free, 250-year-life paper
Manufactured in the United States of America

To the memory of
Walery Wegner

CONTENTS

Secondary Sources

ILLUSTRATIONS

PREFACE

Before I even contemplated this project, I had unwittingly taken a step in its preparation. In 1973, I received as a gift a copy of Daniel Berrigan's *Selected and New Poems* and lost little time acquainting myself with the writing of this priest-activist. As a student in a Catholic high school and college during the Vietnam era, I had heard the name "Berrigan" used as both an epithet and blessing. Some of us followed the course of the Berrigans' antiwar protest, and liberal nuns actually asked us to "pray for those priests" or to read Daniel's poetry.

Later, as a graduate student in history at a state university, my attention was drawn to the antiwar movement as history. Wanting to write a dissertation that would address a major social question in our culture, I chose to examine the antiwar ideas of the Berrigan brothers. This volume lists the wealth of sources I found.

My quest for sources kept me occupied while at SUNY Binghamton. Interlibrary Loan services got my project off to a good start. Soon I discovered the Berrigan Collection at Cornell University. I ferreted out the major portion of my research there, and supplemented it with materials from James Forest of the Fellowship of Reconciliation, Jonah House, the Josephite Fathers Archives, and the Swarthmore College Peace Collection. More research was completed at Colgate-Rochester Divinity School, Cornell Law School, the New York Public Library, the New York State School of Industrial and Labor Relations at Cornell, Rundel Memorial Library in Rochester, New York, and the University of Rochester. Librarians at dozens of institutions patiently answered my reference questions, and Gary Lepper and Carol Rittner, R.S.M., who had done previous bibliographical work on Daniel Berrigan, generously shared their knowledge with me.

This bibliography lists books and articles by and about Daniel, Philip, and Elizabeth McAlister Berrigan. I have limited the citations to published works because of the enormous quantity of material, especially drafts of poems by Daniel Berrigan. This listing of published works should aid researchers who first wish to familiarize themselves with works that have, for the most part, exerted a more widely felt influence than have many of the unpublished items.

The introduction surveys the lives and writings of the Berrigans in the context of recent United States history. A chronology charts some key events that occurred during the lifetimes of these prolific activists.

The bibliography itself lists separately, in chronological order, works by Daniel, Philip, and Elizabeth McAlister Berrigan. Each section is further subdivided into books, contributions to books, and contributions to periodicals. A special section of secondary works, selectively chosen and annotated, adds a foundation for further research on the Berrigans.

Each entry provides as full a bibliographic citation as possible, as well as information pertaining to illustrations, co-authors, and first lines of poetry. Each book entry is accompanied by a short physical description and printing history, where available. Book entries also provide complete listings of the contents of the books, including first lines of poetry and verse fragments.

The volume concludes with a series of indexes to all books, chapters, articles, and poems listed in the chronological sections. There are also a first-line and title index to Daniel Berrigan's poetry and indexes to secondary sources by author and title.

The arrangement of the volume is such that it should afford both general reader and researcher a clear and simple guide to one corner of recent American cultural life.

Acknowledgments

My Ithaca friends deserve a note of thanks for their support for this project. The help I received from Donald Eddy, Alice Klejment, and James Tyler was critical. Nor have I forgotten the many contributions of Clifford Cockerham, Sarah Elbert, Nancy Huling and Rachelle Moore of Interlibrary Loan at SUNY Binghamton, Joann Sikorski, Carol Stevenson, the Webers, and Susan Wolf. Vassar College provided me with grants-in-aid to cover final typing expenses. The Berrigans have provided the material for the entries in this book.

Poughkeepsie, N.Y.
May 1979

INTRODUCTION

The year 1965 was marked by an upsurge of dissidence within the American Catholic church, as well as by angry protest in black ghettos across the country and a spiraling pledge on the part of the Johnson Administration to win the Vietnam War. Among the most articulate and charismatic of the dissident Catholics were two priest-brothers, Daniel Berrigan, then an editor of *Jesuit Missions*, and Philip Berrigan, a Josephite priest who had worked with blacks in the South for ten years. Both of the brothers, outspoken social critics and strong supporters of the civil rights and antiwar movements, were suddenly transferred that year as a result of their uncompromising position on the Vietnam War.

Earlier that year, Daniel and Philip, who with other Catholics of similar social and religious conviction had participated in the founding of the Catholic Peace Fellowship, an offshoot of A.J. Muste's Fellowship of Reconciliation, had signed a "Declaration of Conscience" against the war. They pledged to counter the immorality of the Vietnam involvement with acts of civil disobedience. The declaration, with their signatures, appeared in the February 1965 issue of the *Catholic Worker*, a radical Catholic newspaper published by Dorothy Day. As American military involvement in Southeast Asia deepened, the Berrigans intensified their campaign against the war.

In the early sixties, while venerable members of the Catholic hierarchy were meeting in Rome at the Second Vatican Council, drawing up a policy of modernization for the church, the Berrigans closely followed the Council's reasoning and pronouncements on such matters as Christian conscience, priestly formation, and modern warfare. They noted a widening gulf between the church's revised thinking on moral questions and the Johnson Administration's foreign policy. Daniel and Philip served as models for others as they tried to seek support for new strains of Catholic social thinking that questioned war and violence as a means to peace and justice.

Philip, an instructor in a Josephite seminary in Newburgh, New York, was suddenly removed from his post in April 1965 after his spirited efforts to convince members of that quiet old Hudson River community to take another look at American participation in the Vietnam War. He hammered his points to audiences: American war efforts were immoral because innocent people were being killed; U.S. foreign policy was tinged with racist viewpoints; concerned Christian citizens must help end the war. His first book, *No More Strangers*, published the month of his transfer to a Baltimore ghetto parish, presented his thoughts on war and racism vigorously to an even wider audience.

Daniel provoked controversy in the church over his eulogy for a young Catholic Worker, Roger Laporte, who had, as an antiwar protest, immolated himself. Daniel refused to call the young man's death a suicide, and shortly after this event, one in a long chain of protest activities, Daniel found himself on a special assignment in Latin America for *Jesuit Missions*. The four-month project kept Daniel away from the growing antiwar movement in New York City for the time, but the trip fueled his energies by providing him with new documentation, based on his travels through the Third World.

Daniel was already familiar to some liberal Catholics for his innovative poetry and thoughtful essays on liturgical renewal and social awareness in the Catholic church. A writer for such journals as *Spirit, Thought, Ave Maria, Critic*, and *Commonweal*, the Jesuit poet had become a cause célèbre among those concerned about freedom of conscience and expression within the American Catholic church. After he departed for Mexico, those sympathetic to his cause placed a full-page protest in the *New York Times*, demanding that he be returned to the United States. Whether one agreed with Daniel's specific views or not, the open letter argued, his freedom to speak and write must be protected. The document spoke in favor of the spirit of Catholic Christianity inspired by the Second Vatican Council.

The Berrigan brothers were neither newcomers nor dabblers in social reform and protest movements. Both parents of Daniel and Philip, despite differences in approach, rooted their sons in a Catholic heritage that preserved a commitment to looking toward Christianity for the solution of social problems. The sons took the example of their parents for inspiration and, independently of them, developed their own way of interpreting the Gospels and living according to them in the modern world.

Thomas Berrigan, an Irish-American worker and father of these priest-activists and of four older sons, dedicated his long life to trade unionism. He had repeatedly agitated for the right of workers to organize and obtain just wages and better working conditions. At the peak of his career, Thomas held an executive office in his union local in Syracuse, and he helped found the first Catholic Interracial Council in that central New York city shortly after World War II.

Their mother, Frida Fromhart Berrigan, who as a child had come to the United States from Germany, instilled a strong sense of Christian values in her sons. Without challenging domesticity or traditionally feminine Christian piety, Frida individually lived the Gospel according to her understanding of it. During the thirties, she tried to ease the suffering of the Depression years by housing and feeding wandering, jobless men. Her life of simple Christian charity left its mark on her priest sons, who, when standing trial for their antiwar offenses against the government, cited their mother's influence as motivation for their acts.

Their Catholic schooling, more precisely, their study of the *Baltimore Catechism*, a book of questions and answers on faith that all young Catholics used in parochial schools in the United States, reinforced their parents' social concerns by providing an inspiring religious idealism. The simple answers were memorized word for word and recited in class. From the catechism, however, children could learn that life, even their own childish routines, had value from God. God had created all things, the book noted, and all creation intrinsically deserved respect as a work of God. Persons resembled God not physically but spiritually, for they possessed a nature that had been created in God's image. Therefore, if the students could follow the implications, even those who might be considered the most lowly creatures in earthly hierarchies merited respect as members of God's community and as images of their Creator. These lessons, if learned well, could have a profound influence over a person's concept of social order.

Neither Catholic schooling nor the models of virtue set by their parents, however, provided Daniel and Philip with a clearly defined method of solving social problems. Their father's life showed a deep concern for the position of working men in America. He expressed his dissatisfaction with government policy and contemporary social conditions through his trade unionism and political dissidence. Quite possibly, he was involved with moderate socialist politics during his years as a railroader in Minnesota. Later he admired Father Charles Coughlin, first a New Dealer, then a vitriolic opponent of Franklin Roosevelt from a right-wing perspective. He too became skeptical of New Deal liberalism. Ultimately, he chose to work within the economic, political, and social structures of capitalist society through his activities on behalf of the American Federation of Labor. Their mother's approach to economic and social dislocation reflected a genuine respect for the Gospel that outweighed any concern for politics or structural changes in society. For her, charity was a personal matter.

Catholicism, then, taught no single way of confronting social malaise. In fact, in America it had often emphasized the otherworldly aspects of its traditions and satisfactions because it was faced with the pressing problem of surviving in alien, and sometimes hostile, surroundings. In spite of the guidance of the Gospel, the catechism, the Mass, the sacraments, and the enrichment of the workings of the Spirit in their lives, Catholics could rely on no easy formulas to help them discern the direction of religious and social activism in their lives. For Catholics, conscience defined the extent of one's social concern.

Finally, the brothers' priestly experiences and their dialogue with each other on the meaning of the priesthood led to an additional affirmation that as Christians they needed to be both

contemplatives and social activists in order to fulfill the require-
ments of the law of love. Two strains of thinking had emerged
within the priestly tradition of Catholicism. Monks, who were
largely responsible for preserving the Christian cultural heritage
of the Middle Ages, performed their duties with particular em-
phasis on spiritual matters. Their vocation emphasized solitude,
prayer, and removal from the vices and petty distractions of the
world. Missionaries, on the other hand, who preserved and
nourished the Gospel message to go out and teach all nations,
represented the Christian imperative that one must work in this
world to bring God to all persons. Daniel and Philip tried to
synthesize the monastic and missionary traditions of Catholicism
within the priesthood.

Daniel had entered the Society of Jesus in 1939, after com-
pleting high school, and was formed into a Jesuit priest by the
rigors of Ignatius Loyola's *Spiritual Exercises*, a month-long series
of meditations that encourages persons to give their services
fully and freely to God. The Jesuits had a distinguished history
of worldly activity, which included the labors of Francis Xavier in
Asia and Isaac Jogues and companions in the New World; the
order has been recognized especially for its educators. As a
young seminarian and priest, Daniel taught in Jesuit preparatory schools in Jersey City and Brooklyn before becoming a
professor of dogmatic theology at LeMoyne College in Syracuse.
His Jesuit education would later encourage him to teach Christian social awareness and commitment to all who would listen,
not only in the classroom, but at home or in prison as well. His
teaching methods would cultivate a socially conscious lifestyle,
public exposure, and intensive writing of poetry and short prose
pieces.

Philip, after serving overseas in World War II and finishing
college at Holy Cross, a Jesuit institution, entered the Society of
Saint Joseph, a religious order dedicated to serving black
Catholics. The Josephites provided opportunities for missionary
activity within the United States, for the order built churches
and schools in black areas of Baltimore and Washington as well
as in the bayou country of Louisiana and the tiny outposts in the

rural Delta region of Mississippi. Philip's first assignments sent him to a parish in Washington and a high school in New Orleans. His training had emphasized living a life of poverty and continued social work in the face of strong opposition.

Both Daniel and Philip, fired by religious zeal and their family's advocacy of social awareness, devoted themselves to promoting social change while engaging in full-time teaching and writing. In the early fifties, when Daniel was studying in France, he had come in contact with priests associated with the worker-priest movement. These men of God exchanged their vestments for work clothes, labored beside French workers, and joined with them in strikes in an effort to improve working conditions and bring workers and the Catholic church closer to each other. Daniel enthusiastically wrote about this movement to his seminarian brothers, Jerome and Philip, and to other members of his family. He returned to the United States in 1954 and was assigned by his order to teach at a Jesuit preparatory school in Brooklyn. There, Daniel preached sermons advocating social justice and explained to working-class Catholics how the Mass was an integral part of their lives. He formed young people into groups of Young Christian Workers, worked in Puerto Rican and black ghettos, and campaigned for open housing.

Philip directed much energy into direct action against racial discrimination through his activities for the Congress of Racial Equality (CORE), the Urban League, and the Student Nonviolent Coordinating Committee (SNCC). He and Daniel exchanged notes on social issues and theology, and, when possible, worked together on such projects as the recruitment of black students for northern colleges.

The confluence of religious, social, and artistic direction in the lives of the Berrigans was particularly pronounced even in Daniel's early volumes of collected poetry. *Time Without Number* (1957), Daniel's first book and winner of the Lamont Poetry Award, dealt in largely metaphysical terms with the penetration of spiritual energy into the secular order. His orientation possibly reflected his closeness to the rigors of classical philosophy and theology during his strict thirteen-year formation as a

Jesuit priest. In "The Poet to Himself" and "Each Day Writes,"
Daniel wrote that his struggles as a man trying to lead a Christian
life would direct his poetic imagination, and the volume, as well
as his life, has kept sight of this goal. "Exaltavit Humiles" ad-
dressed the question of the goodness of all God's creation, as did
"I Am Renewed."

He continued his translation of Jesuit spirituality and
modern French theology into a way of life in his two earliest
theological works, *The Bride: Essays in the Church* (1959) and *The
Bow in the Clouds: Man's Covenant with God* (1961). Both works
presented the theme that each individual can use grace and
power to influence the course of secular history. In *Encounters*
(1960), a little-known collection of poetry, Daniel focused on
crisis as a time for religious renewal and commitment among
great figures in the Judeo-Christian religious tradition. Moving
from the metaphysical world of imagery toward a style still
marked by poetic economy, but relying more heavily on imagery
of daily life, Daniel's third volume of poetry, *The World for Wedding Ring* (1962), gave a clearer portrait of his dedication to the
outcast and forgotten. He expressed this concern in his dedication to three persons in the Catholic Worker movement, as well
as in the content of some of his poems, most notably "The Sacraments Are on Behalf of Man," "Having Endured the Dead,"
and "The Face of Christ." These works underscored his personal
commitment to a life of prayer and social activism, and strongly
proclaimed the inseparability of the two.

During the early sixties, the brothers had sought permission
from their religious orders to go on "freedom rides" in the
South, in the hope of promoting racial equality through Christian witness. Their example, perhaps falling short of their particular goal because of the caution of their religious superiors,
continued to demonstrate a Christian witness and encouraged
others to act on behalf of the same causes. The buildup of American military efforts in Southeast Asia, however, channelled the
energies of the two brothers during the mid-sixties. They began
to see that war embodied the same issues as the struggle for civil
rights in America, but in a more comprehensive and urgent way:

they understood that the Vietnam War encompassed the problem of racism. Philip's first book, *No More Strangers* (1965), drew attention to the underlying attitudes in American society that gave rise to both the problems of the segregation of the races and the arms struggle. The work, which reflected Philip's wide reading, was a bold study of social questions in a religious context, and included an introduction by the distinguished Trappist writer, Thomas Merton, who is widely known for his autobiographical work, *The Seven Storey Mountain*.

Shortly after Daniel's assignment to Latin America, two of his works were released, a volume of poetry, *No One Walks Waters*, and *They Call Us Dead Men* (1966). The book of poetry featured a series of poems inspired by Daniel's European sabbatical in 1963–1964, especially in his "Paris Suite" verses. He also included in that slender volume an unmistakable message against the Vietnam War efforts of the Johnson Administration. Despite the church's unfavorable attitude toward his views on the war, Daniel managed to dedicate his book to some associates at the Fellowship of Reconciliation, a Christian pacifist group, and to include a poem he called "Holy Week, 1965 (The Vietnam Raids Go On)." The second work, drawing upon Daniel's thoughtful study of the Pauline tradition in Christian history, indicated that he and his brother rooted their religious radicalism in the tradition of the early church. They would not popularize the growing trend of secularism that marked Christian thinking in the United States during the sixties. Instead, Daniel and Philip aimed at revitalizing Catholic thought by reflecting on the teachings of the early church, and noting how those teachings could be a source for the church to become socially and morally aware of current problems in a competitive, consumer-oriented culture. Again, Daniel presented an antiwar message in the form of a poem dedicated to his friends, peace activists Jim and Sally Douglass, "Peacemaking Is Hard," and in an essay, "Man's Spirit and Technology." He also discussed Christian poverty, marriage, liturgical renewal, and lay leadership within the Catholic church. *Consequences: Truth and . . .* (1967), fruit of Daniel's "exile" to Latin America, was the first volume he wrote while literally on the run. In a series of meditations, Daniel presented prayerful insights into human life as influenced by travels to Selma, Alabama, for a civil rights demonstration, to Sharpeville, South Africa, during his sabbatical, and to Latin America.

As the war in Southeast Asia dragged on, and as Daniel and Philip involved themselves more deeply in acts of protest against it, their writings reflected the urgency of the situation and their resolve to continue raising moral questions concerning the war. In Baltimore in a ghetto parish, Philip increasingly devoted his talents to protesting American involvement in Southeast Asia. With artist Tom Lewis, Philip founded the Baltimore Interfaith Peace Mission and began to protest the war in front of the homes of high government officials and on government property. By 1967 the war had so thoroughly radicalized him that he and three others joined together in Baltimore to seize draft files and pour blood over them. Days before, Daniel and a group of students from Cornell University had been arrested in a protest at the Pentagon. The following spring, the brothers joined with seven others in what became known as the Catonsville Nine action, in which they poured homemade napalm over draft files and set them on fire while they prayed. So electrifying was this act of civil disobedience that over the next several years it would be repeated again and again by other protesters. The draft-board raids solidified the intent of many members of the antiwar movement to commit acts of civil disobedience that challenged the right of property to take precedence over life.

Through these experiences in the antiwar movement, Daniel and Philip emerged as leading Catholic intellectuals who tried a variety of symbolic weapons against the war in the hope of reaching an audience that would likewise refuse to give silent consent to the war. Daniel's *Love, Love at the End* (1968) spoke a message of Christian love, witness, and nonviolence in a collection of witty, ironic, and tragic parables, prayers, and meditations. At the time of its publication, Daniel was in North Vietnam with historian Howard Zinn on a peace mission that arranged the release of three captured American fliers. *Night Flight to Hanoi* (1968) told the story of the pilots' release and the experience of

American bombing in North Vietnam as reported by Daniel in his diary; the volume also included eleven poems. *False Gods, Real Men* (1969) drew together Daniel's experiences in the anti-war struggle from the mid-sixties to the trial of the Catonsville Nine in October 1968. These poems, terse, yet vivid in imagery, unflinchingly confronted the war and resistance to it. "False Gods, Real Men" explained Daniel's view of value changes within his family, and "To the Jesuits" interpreted his feelings toward the religious order that he had entered thirty years before.

While in prison, Daniel and Philip continued to use their literary gifts, and their combined efforts produced more than ten volumes of nonfiction, poetry, drama, conversations, and diaries that directly related their social criticism to their experience. Philip's second major work on racism and war, *A Punishment for Peace* (1969), and his prison musings, *Prison Journals of a Priest Revolutionary* (1970), clarified his political positions against the war and suggested possible ways to end the rule of technological weaponry over human beings.

While serving his prison sentence for the Catonsville action, Daniel received the Frederick Melcher Award (for religious liberalism) for three works that appeared in 1970: *No Bars to Manhood*, essays on nonviolence and radical Christianity in relation to Black Power, the student movement, and the war; *Trial Poems*, a brief collection of poems first published in *False Gods, Real Men*, copied out and illustrated in prison by artist-activist Tom Lewis of the Baltimore Four and Catonsville Nine; and *The Trial of the Catonsville Nine*, Daniel's dramatic rendering of the federal trial, based on the transcript of the court. The play, his most influential and powerful statement against the war, was later produced on stage and adapted for film.

In 1970, to further protest the war, unjust laws, and a severe prison sentence for their act of civil disobedience, Daniel and Philip refused to go directly to jail. They first went underground for a time; Daniel managed to elude his pursuers for four months, although he surfaced from time to time to deliver a sermon or make a statement. Daniel's conversations on Christianity and politics, taped while underground, with psychiatrist

Robert Coles, the raw material for *The Geography of Faith* (1971), contained some insight into the differences between Coles's liberal Catholicism and Daniel's radical Catholicism. He continued his thoughts on radical religion and resistance in *The Dark Night of Resistance* (1971), winner of a National Book Award; consisting of short pieces and poems written while underground, this book illustrated the essential unity of Daniel's prose and poetry styles. *America Is Hard to Find* (1972), an assortment of letters, notes, poems, and talks, presented a personal side of Daniel that previously had been most evident in his poetry, not his prose. He discussed why his antiwar activities had taken a new turn since the Catonsville trial: the new objective of the Berrigans was resistance to the evil policies of the government. Later, both Daniel and Philip would call themselves "anarchists."

The brothers' experiences in federal prisons, and their deepened awareness of the oppressions of American society, have been explored in four works. Philip's *Widen the Prison Gates* (1973) also dealt with federal charges against Philip and his wife, Elizabeth McAlister, concerning a conspiracy to kidnap Henry Kissinger and bomb heating tunnels in government buildings. Daniel's *Absurd Convictions, Modest Hopes* (1972) recorded conversations with journalist Lee Lockwood. *Prison Poems* (1973) contained Daniel's poems about his incarceration in Danbury. He provided new autobiographical material in the lengthy "My Father." "A Prayer to the Blessed Trinity" mocked those who, instead of worshiping the true God, set up their own idols, symbolized by General Motors (Father), General Foods (Son), and General Electric (Spirit). *Lights On in the House of the Dead* (1974), a diary, concluded Daniel's prison writings.

Marking Daniel's popularity as an antiwar poet and activist, Doubleday published an anthology of Daniel's poems, *Selected and New Poems* (1973). The volume contained generous selections from previously published works, some with minor revisions by the author.

Philip Berrigan and Elizabeth McAlister publicly announced their marriage in 1973, after Philip's release from prison. At that time, they set up Jonah House, a resistance commune in Baltimore. Since her marriage, Elizabeth, formerly a religious sister and professor of art history, has begun to write on questions relating to the formation of Christian community. Her writing, often inspired by a biblical text, is marked by its homiletic style. In "Feminists for Life?" (1974) and "A Prison Letter: Raising Children, Resistance, Community" (1977), she has raised important questions about how Christian women might best serve the needs of the resistance movement.

Jesus Christ (1973), a collection of radical interpretations of the meaning of Christ's life and death, presented provocative, often disturbing meditations written by Daniel and illustrated in a crucifix motif by Gregory and Deborah Harris. This work focused on the Christ-centeredness of radical Catholicism, as did *The Raft Is Not the Shore* (1975). In that work, a dialogue between Daniel and Thich Nhat Hanh, a Buddhist monk, the men explored religious consciousness and conscience relating to government, politics, economics, and resistance. In *A Book of Parables* (1977), Daniel retold stories of the Old Testament to appeal to modern sensibilities and to address current moral issues. He rewrote forty psalms and interpreted them briefly in *Uncommon Prayer* (1978), which included Robert McGovern's artistic interpretation of Daniel's poems. *Beside the Sea of Glass* (1978), published only in paperback, discussed a brief passage from the Book of Revelation, and was illustrated with photographs by Frank Kostyu. *The Words Our Savior Gave Us* (1978), also published only in paperback, took a new look at each passage of the Lord's Prayer. Philip's *Of Beasts and Beastly Images* (1979), a collection of essays, advocated resistance to the buildup of nuclear arms.

The earliest of the Berrigan writings differ in politics and tone from the more recent ones, yet all have emphasized the value of human life and the possibilities for radical social change with God's grace. No study of contemporary Catholic culture can ignore the contributions of the Berrigans to politics, religion, and literature.

CHRONOLOGY

1921

9 May   Daniel Berrigan (DB) is born in Virginia, Minnesota.

1923

5 October   Philip Berrigan (PB) is born in Two Harbors, Minnesota.

1939

August   DB, age eighteen, enters the Jesuit seminary to prepare for the priesthood.

17 November   Elizabeth McAlister (EM) is born in Montclair, New Jersey.

1942

13 June   DB's first known publication, "Storm Song," a poem, is published in the Jesuit magazine, *America*.

1943–1946   PB enters the service after having begun studies at St. Michael's College, Toronto.

1950

June   PB is graduated from the College of the Holy Cross, and following in his brother Jerome's steps, he enters the seminary to become a Josephite priest.

1952

19 June   DB is ordained a Jesuit priest by Richard Cardinal Cushing.

1953–1954   DB studies in France and briefly serves as a military chaplain in Germany.

1955

3 June   PB is ordained a Josephite priest, and is assigned to a parish in Washington, D.C.

1957

14 April — Pope Pius XII issues a statement condemning the testing of atomic bombs.

October — PB's first known publication, "A Parish Apostolate," is printed in *Worship*.

8 October — DB publishes his first volume of collected poems. *Time Without Number* later wins the 1957 Lamont Poetry Award of the Academy of American Poets.

1959

12 May — DB's first book of theology, *The Bride*, is published by Macmillan. His sister-in-law, Carol Rizzo Berrigan, designs the dust jacket.

1961

20 January — John F. Kennedy, the first Catholic President of the U.S., is inaugurated.

May — The Congress of Racial Equality (CORE) sponsors the first "freedom rides" in the South.

14 May — Pope John XXIII issues the social encyclical "Mater et Magistra."

1962

11 October — The first session of the Second Vatican Council convenes in Rome.

1963

11 April — *L'Osservatore Romano* publishes "Pacem in Terris," Pope John XXIII's plea for individuals and governments to respect human rights.

28 August — 200,000 march on Washington in support of civil rights for blacks; DB and PB attend the march and later report on it in *Continuum*.

1964

July — DB, in Europe on sabbatical, and others found the Catholic Peace Fellowship. After his sabbatical, he does not return to his teaching position at LeMoyne College, but becomes an editor of *Jesuit Missions*.

7 August — Following the Tonkin Gulf incident, Congress passes

the Gulf of Tonkin Resolution, which grants the President power "for all necessary measures" to protect U.S. forces in Southeast Asia.

3 November   Lyndon Johnson is elected President.

1965

February   The *Catholic Worker* publishes "A Declaration of Conscience," signed by DB, PB, and others, which pledges a campaign of civil disobedience as a protest to the Vietnam War.

7 February   U.S. air forces begin the regular bombing of North Vietnam.

August   DB, Abraham Heschel, and Richard Neuhaus found Clergy Concerned About Vietnam, an interdenominational organization.

4 October   In NYC Pope Paul VI addresses the U.N. with a message of peace: "no more war. War never again."

15 October   David Miller, a Catholic Worker and former student of DB, burns his draft card as a protest against the war and against new legislation aimed at curbing draft-card destruction.

21 November   DB is transferred from NYC to Latin America following his funeral statement for Roger Laporte, a young Catholic Worker, who immolated himself in protest of the war.

12 December   Concerned persons sign a full-page open letter to Francis Cardinal Spellman and the Jesuits, which appeared in the *New York Times*. The signers ask for DB's return to the U.S. and his freedom to speak out on social issues.

1966

March   DB is recalled to the U.S.

December   PB and other members of the Baltimore Interfaith Peace Mission begin holding vigils at the homes of Congressmen as a protest against the Vietnam War.

1967

21 October   DB and students from Cornell University are arrested at an antiwar demonstration at the Pentagon.

27 October	PB and three others, after continued actions against the war, raid a Baltimore draft board and pour blood over the files (Baltimore Four).

1968

January–February	Tet offensive occurs.
February	DB and Howard Zinn visit Hanoi and return with three captured American fliers.
31 March	Lyndon Johnson announces a partial bombing halt in Vietnam and that he will not be a candidate for the Presidency.
17 May	DB, PB, and seven others join in a draft-board raid in a Baltimore suburb in which they burn files with homemade napalm while they pray (Catonsville Nine).
7–11 October	Federal trial of the Catonsville Nine takes place.
5 November	Richard Nixon defeats Hubert Humphrey for the Presidency.
10 December	Thomas Merton, Trappist monk, author, pacifist, and close friend of DB and PB, dies in an accident in Bangkok, Thailand.

1969

8 June	Nixon announces the "Vietnamization" of the war. The first group of American troops is withdrawn from Vietnam.

1970

9 April	DB, PB, and other participants in draft-board raids go underground rather than submit to prison authorities and begin their sentences.
17 April	DB surfaces at the "America Is Hard to Find" weekend at Cornell University. In a hall crowded by students and FBI, DB makes his escape in a towering puppet costume of one of the twelve apostles.
30 April	U.S. invades Cambodia.
1 May	Kent State Massacre occurs.
14 May	Jackson State Massacre occurs.

24 June	The Senate repeals the Gulf of Tonkin Resolution.
17 November	FBI Director J. Edgar Hoover accuses the Berrigans and others of a plot to kidnap Henry Kissinger and bomb heating tunnels of government buildings in Washington, D.C.

1971

12 January	PB and EM are indicted in Harrisburg; DB is named an unindicted co-conspirator.
13 June	The *New York Times* begins publication of the Pentagon Papers.
9 August	PB is sent to "the hole" (solitary confinement) for participation in a prison hunger strike.
19 November	Catholic bishops call for an end to the war.

1972

24 January	The conspiracy trial of the Harrisburg Seven begins.
26 January	DB and PB are nominated for a Nobel Peace Prize.
24 February	After serving nineteen months of his sentence, DB is released from Danbury Federal Penitentiary on parole.
5 April	A Harrisburg jury fails to reach a verdict in the Harrisburg Seven conspiracy trial. PB and EM are found guilty of smuggling letters in and out of prison. Three of the four counts against them are later reversed.
8 May	Nixon announces the mining of harbors in North Vietnam.
7 November	Nixon is re-elected, defeating George McGovern.
20 December	PB is released from prison after completing thirty-nine months of his sentence.

1973

27 January	An agreement is signed committing North and South Vietnam and the U.S. to end the war and restore peace.
29 May	PB and EM announce their marriage. They are excommunicated by the Catholic church.

1 August   Unicorn publishes DB's *Prison Poems*, verses written
                while he was in Danbury.

15 August   U.S. ends the bombing of Cambodia.

October   EM (B) publishes her first known article, "Soil for
                Social Change," in *Theology Today*.

1974

9 August   Nixon resigns as President.

16 September   President Gerald Ford offers a plan for conditional
                amnesty to draft resisters and deserters.

1975

30 April   South Vietnam falls to North Vietnamese forces.

18 November   DB and Vietnamese Buddhist monk Thich Nhat Hanh
                publish *The Raft Is Not the Shore*, their conversations
                while in Paris.

THE BIBLIOGRAPHY

DANIEL BERRIGAN
Books

A-1 TIME WITHOUT NUMBER. New York: Macmillan, 1957.

Poems. 8 October 1957. 53 pp. 22 cm. Dust jacket: maroon
on light blue; jacket on 1st edition makes no mention of the
Lamont Award. Publication figures not available. (Winner of
the Lamont Poetry Award; some poems and variants previously
published in *Spirit* and *Thought*. The volume is dedicated to
his parents.)

Contents:

a   STARS ALMOST ESCAPE US, p. 1: They come unwilling
b   THE CRUCIFIX / (for an eighty-sixth birthday), pp. 2-3:
        I remember today a Quebec roadside, the crucifix
c   THE POET TO HIMSELF, p. 4: Color it not kind
d   PENTECOST, p. 5: All their lives rounded in a backcountry
        brogue
e   THE AUNT, p. 6: With eyes a dying candle
f   THE COAT, p. 7: This is the coat His bowed mother fitted
g   ITS PERFECT HEART, p. 8: It was November: an invisible
        fire
h   THE MOON, p. 9: This desolate cold god
i   CREDENTIALS, p. 10: I would it were possible to state in
        so
j   JUBILEE, p. 11: We stepped down fifty years of path:
        narrow
k   BIRCHES, p. 12: Lovely their plumage grew: when winds
        bore down,
l   EVERYTHING THAT IS, p. 13: is not something other:
m   OVER SODDEN ANONYMOUS FIELDS, p. 14: suddenly from trees
        that had awaited
n   HERE THE STEM RISES, p. 15: deflowered forever.
o   IN THE GRAVE LENTEN TIME, p. 16: when snow wept from the
        lime

A-2: dust jacket by Carol Rizzo Berrigan

A-2 THE BRIDE: Essays in the Church. New York: Macmillan, 1959.

Essays. 12 May 1959. 123 pp. 22 cm. Dust jacket: dark green on light green; illustration by Carol Rizzo Berrigan, wife of the author's brother Jerome. Publication figures not available. (Some of the material has been reworked from publications in the *Modern Humanist*. The dedication is to the author's brother, Philip.)

Contents:

a   INTRODUCTION, pp. 1-8
b   I.   ISRAEL, pp. 9-13
c   II.   THE EVENT, pp. 14-23
d   III.   BEGINNINGS, pp. 24-32
e   IV.   ALL THINGS NEW, pp. 33-41
f   V.   PERSON, pp. 42-51
g   VI.   TASK, pp. 52-63
h   VII.   SUFFERING, pp. 64-76
i   VIII. PRAYER, pp. 77-90
j   IX.   THE SACRIFICE, pp. 91-101
k   X.   FULNESS, pp. 102-116
l   XI.   THE KINGDOM, pp. 117-128
m   XII.   THE SAINTS, pp. 129-137
n   XIII. UNTIL HE COME, pp. 138-142

A-3 ENCOUNTERS. Cleveland: World Publishing, 1960.

Poems. 15 February 1960. 76 pp. 21 cm. Dust jacket: black lettering and color photograph on glossy white. Publication figures not available. (Some poems previously published in *Poetry*, *Commonweal*, *America*, *Thought*.)

Contents:

a   EVE, p. 13: It was for love of me
b   ABEL, p. 14: One blood veined us, stem and fruit
c   NOE, p. 15: Whispered to me: will you mount the waters?
d   ABRAHAM, p. 16: To see my small son
e   ISAAC, p. 17: My heart slows to my father's
f   JOB, p. 18: I stood sons up like shields, leather and
       bone
g   ELIAS, p. 19: Childhood I stumbled through, a sleepwalker
h   EZECHIEL, p. 20: Forest cut off at youth's high tide
i   CHRIST, p. 21: Words are outer form
j   MARY, p. 22: Offer a time when Christ's mother's name
k   SAINT ANN / (*who bore a daughter in late life*), p. 23:
       Hand that folded and laid aside my fabric
l   SAINT JOSEPH / I, p. 24: One corner of field my plow
       veered from

at DOMES, p. 62: that raise the improbable to an art,
au MORE LIKE THE SEA / (A man is more than two sticks
       crossed. / He is more like the sea, bringing up God
       knows what / at any moment: Conrad.), p. 63: Nail him
       to sticks
av RADICAL STRENGTH, p. 64: issues in marvels:
aw CHILD ABOVE A FLOWER, p. 65: unsure
ax WE LOVE, p. 66: about trees: past is never tall enough,
ay TASKS, p. 67: Hercules strides back from hell, bearing
az GO DOWN ON KNEE, p. 68: I saw an old wife stricken, the
       man
ba TO A PRAGMATIST, IN DEATH, p. 69: Offer a flower
bb CHARTRES, p. 70: Night to quiet countryside comes. The
       cathedral
bc THIRST, p. 71: In him no beauty was
bd HOW LARGE, p. 72: a lark must be
be LITERAL, p. 73: is the wing's breadth that dares
bf A VOICE OF LEAVES, p. 74: Even to be a tree, erect and
       generous
bg LATE, p. 75: I follow stumbling Jesus down the wall:
bh THIS BOOK BEARS, p. 76: like a good voyager, marks of
       passage:

A-4 THE BOW IN THE CLOUDS: Man's Covenant With God. New
York: Coward-McCann, 1961.

Essays. 27 November 1961. 220 pp. 22 cm. Dust jacket:
black and white design on red by Irene Murray. 5000 printed,
4000 bound, 1000 destroyed. (Dedicated to Sister Maria
Josephine Berrigan, aunt of the author.)

Contents:

     PART I

a   1. THE FALL, pp. 13-29
b   2. ABRAHAM AND THE MAN OF FAITH, pp. 30-52
c   3. IMAGINATION AND COVENANT, pp. 53-77
d   4. PROPHECY AND SOCIETY, pp. 78-104
e   5. ALL THINGS NEW, pp. 105-122

     PART II

f   1. THE CHRISTIAN AND CREATION, pp. 125-147
g   2. INCARNATION AND APOSTOLATE, pp. 148-170
h   3. THE FIRST NEW MEN: THE TWELVE, pp. 171-183
i   4. CATHOLICISM AND THE INTELLIGENCE, pp. 184-201
j   5. SACRIFICE AND MAN'S HOPE, pp. 202-220

A-5 THE WORLD FOR WEDDING RING. New York: Macmillan, 1962.

Poems. 12 November 1962. 77 pp. 22 cm. Dust jacket:
black, gray, and pink design on white by Hermann Strohbach.
Photograph of author on back. Publication figures not available. (Some poems printed originally in *America*, *The American Scholar*, *Commonweal*, *Poetry*, *Spirit*, *Thought*, and *Unity*.
Dedicated to Dorothy Day, Tony Walsh, and Karl Meyer.)

Contents:

A-6 ENCOUNTERS. Associated American Artists. New York:
1965.

Poems. Date of publication not available. Unpaginated. 9
plates in portfolio. 40 cm. Illustrations by Robert E. Marx.
75 copies. (Contains poems selected from *Encounters*, 1960.)

Contents:

a   I FACES: Flower bears flower interminably.
b   III CHILD ABOVE A FLOWER: unsure
c   V CHORALE: as though time fitted them
d   VII RECOLLECTION: I love aftermath of action: the mind's
e   IX REACHING TO QUENCH A LIGHT AT MIDNIGHT: Perhaps light
f   XI AN OLD WOMAN IN DEATH: For *words words* death's
        instantaneous
g   XIII VOCATION: Hemlocks in row, heads bowed beneath
        snowfall

A-7 NO ONE WALKS WATERS. New York: Macmillan, 1966.

Poems. 21 February 1966. 78 pp. 22 cm. Dust jacket: white
and black lettering on blue and white by Corita Kent. Publication figures not available. (Some poems previously published in *Ave Maria*, *Commonweal*, *Thought*, *Sponsa Regis*, *Wood-
stock Letters*, *Continuum*, *Spirit*, *Catholic Worker*, *Christian
Century*, *Today*, *Motive*, and *Poetry*. Dedicated to John and
Elizabeth Heidbrink and the Fellowship of Reconciliation.)

Contents:

a   HOLY WEEK, 1965 / (THE VIETNAM RAIDS GO ON) [p. vii]:
        For us to make a choice
b   THE BOOK, p. 1: A living eye rested on the book,
c   THE WRITING OF A POEM, p. 2: The greatness of art
d   KEEP THE HOUR, p. 3: I set this down toward May midnight.
e   WEDDING, pp. 4-5: The mind,
f   UNFINISHED, p. 6: The world is somewhere visibly round,
g   THE KINGS CAME BEARING GIFTS, p. 7: Were there humans
        worthy of it,
h   HENRY MOORE IN THE GARDEN, p. 8: The hard wrought face
i   WE ARE IN LOVE, THE CELIBATES GRAVELY SAY, p. 9: They
        hold Christ up for ascension
j   THE LEPER, pp. 10-11: In the torrid breathless noon
k   THE QUESTION, p. 12: If the world's temperate zone,
l   MIRACLES, p. 13: Were I God almighty, I would ordain,

au HOW STRANGE THE WORLD, p. 54: Richness, strangeness,
     depth; I see
av DACHAU IS NOW OPEN FOR VISITORS, p. 55: The arabesque
     scrawled by the dead
aw IN THE CHILDREN'S WARD, p. 56: I was pondering no mystery
ax I FEAR MOST, I THINK, p. 57: if nightmare is oracle--
ay COMPASSION, p. 58: I sing bronze statuary
az PARIS SUITE [A series of 12 numbered poems, pp. 61-73.
     Individual entries follow.]
     1. A BEGGAR, FIRST, p. 61: Sometimes, misery has beauty
          to commend it.
     2. OUR LADY OF PARIS, p. 62: The mother, frail seeming
          as flesh
     3. CERTAIN CONCESSIONS, p. 63: You are not the golden
          Greek sea, no
     4. UNFINISHED LINES, p. 64: October scuds; leaves come
          down
     5. SAINT SULPICE, p. 65: In the botched barracks, coming
          on
     6. A VIEW FROM A SIDE STREET, p. 66: The streets shoul-
          dering awkwardly along
     7. THE CITY UNDERTAKES A RESTORATION OF PUBLIC MONUMENTS,
          p. 67: How much life do you allow us?
     8. PARIS, YOU COULD PRESS WINE FROM THISTLES, p. 68:
          make easter eggs of gutter stones.
     9. THE NEWS STAND, p. 69: In cold November
     10. A THRUSH IN THE CITY, p. 70: Supple as a fish
     11. IMMANENCE, p. 71: I see You in the world--
     12. AIR MAIL LETTER, pp. 72-73: A brutal landscape
ba THE TEST, p. 74: With serious intent, He created
bb MAKING SOMETHING, p. 75: The blind man longed passionately
     to see
bc FORTY-TWO, p. 76: Come passionately into life,
bd THE JEWEL / (AT A LECTURE), p. 77: The lady wore a jewel
be THIS BOOK, p. 78: As I walk patiently through life

A-8 THEY CALL US DEAD MEN: Reflections on Life and Conscience. New York: Macmillan, 1966.

Essays. 21 February 1966. 192 pp. 22 cm. Dust jacket:
Black and yellow lettering and design on white by Corita Kent.
Publication figures not available. Paperback edition pub-
lished by Macmillan. (Some pieces previously published in
Fellowship, *Grail International Review*, *Liturgical Conference*,
Perspectives, *Worldview*, and *Worship*. Dedicated to Jim and
Sally Douglass.)

Contents:

a   [PEACEMAKING IS HARD] / [to Jim and Sally Douglass], p. [5]:
       Peacemaking is hard
b   INTRODUCTION BY WILLIAM STRINGFELLOW, pp. 11-13
c   1. POVERTY AND THE LIFE OF THE CHURCH, pp. 15-32
d   2. MARRIAGE, pp. 33-48
e   3. THE ETERNAL YOUTH OF THE CHURCH, pp. 49-68
f   4. THE PRIESTHOOD OF THE LAITY, pp. 69-88
g   5. SACRED ART AND THE LIFE OF MAN, pp. 89-101
h   6. NOTES ON RENEWAL, pp. 102-120
i   7. ST. PAUL: FIGURE OF CRISIS, pp. 121-155
j   8. MAN'S SPIRIT AND TECHNOLOGY, pp. 156-172
k   9. NEW WORLD, NEW FORMS OF FAITH, pp. 173-192

A-9   THE WORLD SHOWED ME ITS HEART.   St. Louis: National
Sodality Service Center, 1966.

Essays reprinted in pamphlet form.   Date of publication not
available.   27 pp.   20 cm.   (Essays were previously published
in *Queen's Work*.)

Contents:

a   FOREWORD BY JOSEPH F. MacFARLANE, S.J., p. 5
b   THE WORLD SHOWED ME ITS HEART, pp. 6-27

A-10   CONSEQUENCES: TRUTH AND...   New York: Macmillan, 1967.

Meditations.   3 April 1967.   123 pp.   21 cm.   Dust jacket:
white and red lettering on dark green background by Corita
Kent.   (Variants published in *Commonweal* and *Jubilee*.   Dedicated to Jerry and Carol [Berrigan].)

Contents:

a   DEDICATION: *JERRY* AND *CAROL*-- TO SAY I LOVE YOU, pp. v-ix
b   JOURNEY TOWARD FIDELITY, pp. 1-62
c   JOURNEY FROM SHARPEVILLE TO SELMA, pp. 63-73
d   TO LIMBO AND BACK: A LATIN AMERICAN JOURNEY, pp. 75-123

A-10: dust jacket by Corita Kent

A-11: dust jacket by Corita Kent

A-11 LOVE, LOVE AT THE END. New York: Macmillan, 1968.

Parables, prayers, and meditations in prose and poetry.
26 February 1968. 118 pp. 21 cm. Dust jacket: black lettering and red lettering and design on white background by Corita
Kent. Publication figures not available. Paperback edition
published by Macmillan. (Some material previously printed
in *Critic* and *National Catholic Reporter*. Dedicated to Jack
and Mary Lewis.)

Contents:

    I PARABLES

a   NO CUTTING LOOSE, pp. 3-4
b   IRENE, pp. 5-6
c   MY SON JOHN, pp. 7-9
d   DEATH AND THE BISHOP, pp. 10-11
e   THE SAD ONE, p. 12
f   THE BOY AND THE TIGER, pp. 13-15
g   PLEASE, PLEASE, p. 16
h   THE TOOLS, pp. 17-19
i   THE CATECHUMENS, pp. 20-22
j   ALLELUIA, pp. 23-24
k   THE SINGLE ROSE, pp. 25-26
l   ALAS, p. 27
m   THE SHOES THAT FAILED, pp. 28-29
n   THE TEMPTER, pp. 30-31
o   THE EDGE, pp. 32-33
p   THE FIRST DAYS OF THE SCIENCE OF PRENATAL COMMUNICATION,
        pp. 34-36
q   PRAY TOGETHER--STAY TOGETHER, pp. 37-39
r   THE YOUNG SHEPHERD, pp. 40-43
s   THE ZOO KEEPER, pp. 44-46
t   DAY OF JUDGMENT, pp. 47-49
u   THE BOX, pp. 50-51
v   HOPE, OR ALL IS NOT LOST BUT ALMOST ALL, pp. 52-54
w   THE STATUE, pp. 55-57
x   MADAME ZERO, pp. 58-59
y   THE BOAT, pp. 60-62
z   FAIRY TALE, p. 63
aa   THE BIRD, pp. 64-65
ab   THE DREAM, pp. 66-67
ac   ONE MAN, pp. 68-69
ad   THE COMMUTER, pp. 70-72
ae   TWO SOLDIERS, pp. 73-78
af   NO HUMANS ON FRIDAY, pp. 79-82

II PRAYERS

III MEDITATIONS

A-12 NIGHT FLIGHT TO HANOI: War Diary with 11 Poems. New
York: Macmillan, 1968.

Diary with poems. 14 October 1968. 140 pp. 21 cm. Dust
jacket: white and red lettering on black background by Corita
Kent. Publication figures not available. (Some pieces previously published in *Liberation*, *National Catholic Reporter*,
and *Worldview*. Dedicated to author's brother, Philip.)

Contents:

l   SONG, p. 49: The maids sing at their scrubbing
m   NIGHT FLIGHT TO HANOI: SUNDAY, FEBRUARY 11, pp. 50-57
n   CHILDREN IN THE SHELTER, p. 57: Imagine; three of them.
o   NIGHT FLIGHT TO HANOI: MONDAY, FEBRUARY 12, pp. 58-73
p   PROGRESS IN RURAL DEVELOPMENT: A LECTURE ON PRIVIES, AND
        A GIFT TO OUR COUNTRYMEN, p. 60: In the municipal hos-
        pital, in the bone-chilling cold
q   NIGHT FLIGHT TO HANOI: TUESDAY, FEBRUARY 13, pp. 74-96
r   THE PILOTS RELEASED, p. 91: The trouble with innocence
s   NIGHT FLIGHT TO HANOI: WEDNESDAY, FEBRUARY 14, pp. 97-120
t   ALERT, p. 102: The sirens are loosed on Hanoi
u   BOMBARDMENT, p. 113: Like those who go aground
v   NIGHT FLIGHT TO HANOI: THURSDAY, FEBRUARY 15, pp. 121-124
w   NIGHT FLIGHT TO HANOI: FRIDAY, FEBRUARY 16, pp. 125-130
x   NIGHT FLIGHT TO HANOI: FRIDAY EVENING, FEBRUARY 16, pp.
        131-140
y   MY NAME, p. 135: If I were Pablo Neruda
z   THE PILOTS, RELEASED, p. 139: When I think of you it is
        always (forgive me)

A-13 FALSE GODS, REAL MEN. New York: Macmillan, 1969.

Poems. 17 March 1969. 111 pp. 22 cm. Dust jacket: maroon
and white lettering over a black and white photograph by Corita Kent. Publication figures not available. (Some poems
first published in *Epoch*, *Continuum*, *New Yorker*, *Motive*,
Poetry, *Thought*. Dedicated to the Catonsville Nine.)

Contents:

    I "I HAD A SENSE..."

a   FALSE GODS, REAL MEN, pp. 3-7: Our family moved in 25
        years from Acceptable Ethnic
        1. [AMONG THE FLAG POLES]: Among the flag poles
        2. [WE DID YES WE DID YOUR HONOR]: We did yes we did
            your Honor
        3. [WE FOOLS AND FELONS]: We fools and felons
        4. [THEN FOUL MACADAM]: Then foul macadam
        5. [JUDGE MACE HIS BLACK]: Judge Mace his black
        6. [INDICTED]: Indicted
        7. [THE CURE FOR FOUL DREAMS]: The cure for foul dreams
        8. [COMPASSIONATE, CASUAL AS A GOOD FACE] / (TO PHILIP):
            Compassionate, casual as a good face
b   II INTENTIONAL--INDEED WILLFUL, p. 9
c   WAITING: VIETIANE, p. 11: The birds of dawn are crying,
        drawing

bq   BREAD, p. 95: A loaf of it shaped like God
br   BUTTERFLY, p. 96: Wrapped like dead Jesus in 1) the
        American flag
bs   SUBWAY, p. 97: The worm is full of people, death
        reversed!

        VII   HORATIO...

bt   HORATIO: A SHORT SNAPPY LIFE, p. 99: Horatio: a Short
        Snappy Life
bu   BABY, p. 101: I pushed out of there on my tricycle
bv   PLAY, p. 102: Said to me sternly; play the game!
bw   HEART, p. 103: When I was a city kid, we had a game
bx   SUN, p. 104: *always comes on strong*
by   GOD, p. 105: Lined up like easter eggs
bz   HOLIDAY, p. 106: One July
ca   CITY, p. 107: Imagine a Toltec city
cb   SMILE, p. 108: Not round enough
cc   MY GUTS BEGIN, p. 109: like white trash
cd   SEX, p. 110: When I was 48
ce   DEATH, p. 111: He was on stilts

A-14   NO BARS TO MANHOOD.   Garden City, N.Y.: Doubleday, 1970.

Essays.   20 March 1970.   215 pp.   22 cm.   Dust jacket: yellow,
red, white, and black lettering and a blue and yellow design
on white background by Jay J. Smith Studio.   Photograph of
author on back by John Dejournett.   Doubleday edition: 7,500
copies.   Paperback edition published by Bantam: 195,500 copies.   (Some pieces previously printed in *Continuum*, *Critic*,
Jesuit Missions, *Katallagete*, *Motive*, *National Catholic Reporter*, and *U.S. Catholic*.   Dedicated to author's father and
Thomas Merton.)

Contents:

        PART ONE: A SPIRITUAL GEOGRAPHY

PART TWO: PROPHETS AND PRISONERS

PART THREE: CORNELL

EPILOGUE

A–15   THE TRIAL OF THE CATONSVILLE NINE. Boston: Beacon
Press, 1970.

Verse play with poems.   14 April 1970.   122 pp. 21 cm. Dust
jacket: orange and deep red design and lettering by Corita
Kent. Publication figures not available. Published in paperback by Beacon and Bantam.   (Dedicated to David Darst, deceased member of the Catonsville Nine.)

Contents:

A-16   TRIAL POEMS.   Boston: Beacon Press, 1970.

Poems.   14 April 1970.   Unpaginated.   34 cm.   Dust jacket:
black design and lettering on red background.   Publication
figures not available.   (A facsimile edition of prison poems
by Daniel Berrigan copied out and illustrated by Thomas Lewis.)

Contents:

a   INTRODUCTION by Thomas Lewis, pp. [iii-iv]
b   [IN BALTIMORE AS WE CAME IN FOR TRIAL], p. [5]: In Balti-
       more as we came in for trial
c   [FOR THE CONSTRUCTION, OUTFITTING AND MAINTENANCE OF A
       FEDERAL COURT OF JUSTICE], p. [7]: For the construction,
       outfitting and maintenance of a federal court of justice
d   [THE MARSHAL IS TAKING MY MEASURE], p. [9]: The marshal is
       taking my measure
e   [IN OUR BIG CRUEL WARD], p. [11]: In our big cruel ward
f   [SUPERSONIC TIME], p. [15]: Supersonic time
g   [I LONGED ONCE, IN THE WORSE DAYS], p. [17]: I longed
       once, in the worse days
h   [WE SIT OR WALK OUR CAGE], p. [19]: We sit or walk our
       cage
i   [AT 7 A.M. ON TRIAL DAY], p. [19]: At 7 A.M. on trial day
j   [ALL ELBOWS, CROOKS AND KNEES], pp. [21, 23]: All elbows,
       crooks and knees
k   [THE BOXES OF PAPER ASH], pp. [21, 23]: The boxes of
       paper ash
l   [EVERYTHING BEFORE WAS A GREAT LIE.], p. [25]: Everything
       before was a great lie.

A-17   CRIME TRIAL.   Boston: Impressions Workshop, 1970.

Poems.   Date of publication not available.   Unpaginated portfolio.   40 cm.   90 copies.   (22 poems, some published previously in *False Gods*, *Real Men*, and *Trial Poems*.   13 illustrations by Robert E. Marx.)

Contents:

   CRIME POEMS

a   1. FALSE GODS, REAL MEN: Our family moved in 25 years
          from Acceptable Ethnic through Ideal American
b   2. [AMONG THE FLAG POLES]: Among the flag poles
c   3. [WE DID YES WE DID YOUR HONOR]: We did yes we did
          your Honor

d   4. [WE FOOLS AND FELONS]: We fools and felons
e   5. [THEN FOUL MACADAM]: Then foul macadam
f   6. [JUDGE MACE HIS BLACK]: Judge Mace his black
g   7. [INDICTED]: Indicted
h   8. [THE CURE FOR FOUL DREAMS]: The cure for foul dreams
i   9. [COMPASSIONATE, CASUAL AS A GOOD FACE] / (To Philip):
        Compassionate, casual as a good face

    TRIAL POEMS

j   1. [IN BALTIMORE AS WE CAME IN FOR TRIAL]: In Baltimore
        as we came in for trial
k   2. FOR THE CONSTRUCTION, OUTFITTING AND MAINTENANCE OF A
        FEDERAL COURT OF JUSTICE: No swimming Aloud.
l   3. [THE MARSHAL IS TAKING MY MEASURE]: The marshal is
        taking my measure
m   4. [IN OUR BIG CRUEL CELL BLOCK]: In our big cruel cell
        block
n   5. [SUPERSONIC TIME]: supersonic time
o   6. [I LONGED ONCE, IN THE WORST DAYS,]: I longed once,
        in the worst days,
p   7. [WE SIT OR WALK OUR CAGE]: We sit or walk our cage
q   8. [AT 7 A.M. ON TRIAL DAY]: At 7 a.m. on trial day
r   9. [THE SEXLESS JUDGE, UNDER DECENT BLACK IS]: The sex-
        less judge, under decent black is
s 10. [ALL CREATION]: All creation
t 11. [ALL ELBOWS, CROOKS AND KNEES]: All elbows, crooks
        and knees
u 12. [THE SIZE OF INFANT CASKETS]: the size of infant
        caskets
v 13. [EVERYTHING BEFORE WAS A GREAT LIE.]: Everything
        before was a great lie.

A-18   THE DARK NIGHT OF RESISTANCE. Garden City, N.Y.:
Doubleday, 1971.

Essays and poems. 4 June 1971. 181 pp. 22 cm. Dust jacket:
purple, blue, and green design; white lettering on a black
and white photograph by Corita Kent. Photograph of author on
back by Bob Fitch. 16,000 hardbound copies. Paperback edition
published by Bantam. (Winner of the St. Thomas More book
award. Dedicated to William Stringfellow and Anthony Towne.)

Contents:

a   APRIL 1970, pp. 1-14
b   BY NIGHT I WENT OUT BY THE BACK WINDOW WHILE THE FBI WAS
    FUMBLING AT THE FRONT DOOR, pp. 15-28

c   THE DARK NIGHT OF RESISTANCE, IN WHICH ALL ANTICS, ATTI-
    TUDES, WHISPERINGS, AND ESPECIALLY FREEDOMS AND UNFREE-
    DOMS AND THEIR MIMICS AND GRIMACES, ARE ABROAD; A
    WITCH'S NIGHT, IN SHORT, pp. 29-32

d   FATHERS AND SONS: UTOPIAN PROPOSALS SCRAWLED ON CAVE
    WALLS BY THOSE WHO HAD EVERYTHING TO LOSE, WHOSE HAND
    THEREFORE WAS STEADY AND INVENTIVE, AS IN THE LIGHT,
    pp. 33-38

e   THAT THE MONK AND THE ACTIVIST OUGHT TO SIT DOWN TOGETHER:
    THAT WOULD INDEED BE SOMETHING MORE FOR US THAN THE
    USUAL TAWDRY FANCY FOOTWORK OF HEADS OF STATE OR BODIES
    POLITIC, pp. 39-49

f   CERTAIN OCCULT UTTERANCES FROM THE UNDER GROUND AND ITS
    GUARDIAN SPHINX, pp. 50-51: If you seek pleasure in
    everything

g   KOAN AND COMMENTARY OF THE PRECEDING, pp. 52-58

h   [A BRIEF PAUSE A REFRESHMENT IN THE COURSE OF ...], p. 59:
    A Brief Pause a Refreshment in the Course of

i   LADEN FOG IT IS IN WELCOMING THIS UNIVERSAL ELEMENT WE
    STAND WITHIN REST WITHIN AND RISE EMBOLDENED BY THE
    TRUTH, pp. 60-61: The second part of this night which
    is faith

j   NOW IF YOU WILL PLEASE IN THIS DARKNESS CHOOSE YOUR IMAGE
    OF THE WORLD INHABIT IT WALK WITHIN IT PEACEABLY OR RUN
    LIKE HELL THE OTHER WAY, pp. 62-66

k   A MAN MUST BE LIKE A BLIND MAN FINDING HIS ONLY SUPPORT
    IN DARK FAITH TAKING IT AS HIS LIGHT AND GUIDE AND
    LEANING UPON NONE OF THE THINGS WHICH HE UNDERSTANDS
    ENJOYS FEELS AND IMAGINES, pp. 67-71

l   DARKNESS DARKNESS DARKNESS HOW ABOUT SOME LIGHT?,
    pp. 72-78

m   WHEREIN A SERIES OF CONTRADICTIONS IS POINTED OUT IN VIEW
    PERHAPS OF A RESOLUTION OF TRUTH, pp. 79-85: According
    to practically every Zen master who ever wrote

n   GOD LEADS A MAN STEP BY STEP TO THE GREATEST DEGREE OF IN-
    WARDNESS; OR, SIMPLICITY IS A DIFFERENT MATTER FROM A
    HATFUL OF WATCH PARTS WHICH, GRACE OF A BAVARIAN GRAND-
    PA, HAS BECOME A WATCH, pp. 86-90

o   IN WHICH THE MORAL OF THE PRECEDING IS DISCUSSED, pp.
    91-97

p   CLINGING TO THE HUSK OF SENSE (AN ATTITUDE WHICH RESEMBLES
    THE STATE OF CHILDHOOD) A MAN NEVER ATTAINS TO THE SUB-
    STANCE OF THE SPIRIT (WHICH RESEMBLES THE STATE OF PER-
    FECT MANHOOD), pp. 98-106

q   THE UNDERSTANDING SHOULD NOT FEED UPON VISIONS. BEING A
    MEDITATION ON A SPECIAL EDITION OF *LIFE* MAGAZINE: TO
    THE MOON AND BACK, pp. 107-114

r   [PURSUANT TO ALL OF WHICH], pp. 111-114: I am led to
    Mr. Dickey's poem,

s   THE UNDERSTANDING SHOULD NOT FEED UPON VISIONS CONTINUED.
    THE SUBJECT BEING OF SOME IMPORT TO THE DENIZENS OF
    THESE 50 STATES, THE DISCUSSION CONTINUES, IN SOMEWHAT
    THE FOLLOWING FORM. THE SHADE OF OUR GURU IS SUMMONED,
    pp. 115-121
t   BEING A SUGGESTED BEGINNERS' LIST OF VISIONS THE MIND
    SHOULD NOT FEED UPON, pp. 122-126
u   AND FINALLY A FEW VISIONS WHICH IT IS LAWFUL NAY LAUDABLE
    TO ENTERTAIN, pp. 127-132
v   I AM NOT EVEN SURE THAT THE FOLLOWING IS A VISIONARY
    STATEMENT: DECIDE PLEASE FOR YOURSELF, pp. 133-135:
    Jesus says;
w   IT SEEMS EXPEDIENT TO RETURN TO THE WORDS OF OUR GURU
    HERE APPENDED TOGETHER WITH CERTAIN COMMENTS (WHICH
    LATER MAY BE IGNORED AT WILL), pp. 136-140
x   ONLY A GURU WOULD HAVE DARED WRITE IT: "THE BENEFITS
    WHICH ARISE FROM FORGETFULNESS." WE WILL, AT HIS BE-
    HEST, PURSUE THE SUBJECT, pp. 141-148
y   QUESTION: WHAT THEN IS IT TO REMEMBER? ANSWER: FORGET IT,
    pp. 149-154: One thing you must grant our guru
z   A PENNY PRIMER IN THE ART OF FORGETFULNESS, pp. 155-157:
    What is the price of attaining the future?
aa "NIGHT DARKENS THE SOUL OF MAN: BUT ONLY TO ILLUMINATE IT"
    WORDS ONCE MORE TAKEN FROM THE NOTES OF OUR GURU,
    pp. 158-160: This night darkens the spirit but only to
    illuminate it
ab SOME DEFINITIONS OF FAVORITE RECURRING WORDS OF OUR GURU
    ARE NOW IN ORDER, pp. 161-170
ac TWO TEXTS ARE COMMENDED BY OUR GURU AS COMMENDING A REA-
    SONABLE FREEDOM FROM THE GOODS AND SERVICES OF THIS
    WORLD, pp. 171-176
ad LET A MAN GROUND HIS JOY AND LOVE IN THAT WHICH HE NEI-
    THER SEES NOR FEELS NOR CAN FEEL OR SEE IN THIS LIFE:
    NAMELY IN GOD, pp. 177-181

A-19 THE GEOGRAPHY OF FAITH: Conversations Between Daniel
Berrigan, When Underground, and Robert Coles. Boston: Beacon
Press, 1971.

Conversations. 6 October 1971. 179 pp. 22 cm. Dust jacket:
blue and black design with white and gold and light blue lettering by Richard C. Bartlett. Publication figures not available. Paperback edition published by Beacon. (Some sections
previously appeared in the *New York Review of Books*.)

Contents:

A-20 AMERICA IS HARD TO FIND. Garden City, NY: Doubleday, 1972.

Letters, talks, and poems. 22 September 1972. 191 pp. 22 cm.
Dust jacket: red and green design by Daniel Berrigan, black
and red lettering on white background by Cheryl Brown. Photograph of author on back by Audrey Schirmer. 8,500 copies.
(Some pieces previously published in *Christian Century*, *Commonweal*, *Cornell Sun*, New York *Times*, *Saturday Review*, and
Village Voice.)

Contents:

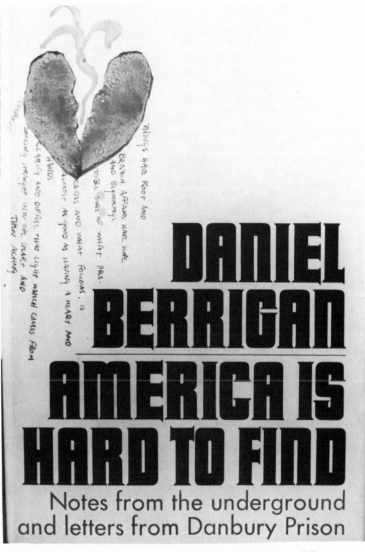

THiNGS HAVE ROOT AND
BRANCH, AFFAIRS HAVE SOME
AND BEGINNINGS
TO BE SURE OF WHAT PRE-
CEDES AND WHAT FOLLOWS, IS
ALMOST AS GOOD AS HAVING A HEART AND
HANDS.
CLARIFY AND DIFFUSE THAT LIGHT WHICH COMES FROM
LOOKING STRAIGHT INTO THE HEART AND
THEN ACTING.

**DANIEL
BERRIGAN
AMERICA IS
HARD TO FIND**

Notes from the underground
and letters from Danbury Prison

A-20: dust jacket by Daniel Berrigan and Cheryl Brown

p   LETTER TO THE WEATHERMEN, pp. 92-98

     III   JAILHOUSE NOTES

q   FIRST LETTER FROM DANBURY, pp. 101-102
r   A SERMON FROM PRISON, pp. 103-107
s   A LETTER TO JUDGE ROSZEL THOMSEN, pp. 108-119
t   A LETTER TO J. EDGAR HOOVER, pp. 120-127
u   LETTER TO THE YOUNG JESUITS, pp. 128-139
v   FAMILY LETTERS, pp. 140-169
w   THE FIRST CRY OF A CHILD / (to our Mother), pp. 170-172:
     like an alert on a silent night
x   ON BEING HERE WITH PHIL / (5/29/71), pp. 173-175: When-
     ever I met a crook here
y   TULIPS IN THE PRISON YARD, p. 176: All kinds of poets,
     believe me, could better praise your
z   [UNTITLED ESSAY], pp. 179-191: [The following essay was
     written in 1969, after the death of David Darst, the
     youngest member of the Catonsville Nine. It is includ-
     ed here because of its relevance to all the preceding
     material.]

A-21 ABSURD CONVICTIONS, MODEST HOPES. Conversations after
Prison with Lee Lockwood. New York: Random House, 1972.

Conversations and poems. Date of publication not available.
227 pp. 22 cm. Dust jacket: rust and blue lettering on white
background with gold rim. Photograph of authors by Paul
Petricone. Publication figures not available. Paperback
edition published by Vintage. (Material not previously
published.)

Contents:

a   INTRODUCTORY NOTE BY LEE LOCKWOOD, pp. ix-xx
b   [UNTITLED POEM] / (APRIL 17, 1971), p. xvii: teach my
     eyes to rejoice in one shivering
c   [UNTITLED POEM] / (MAY 8, 1971), p. xviii: The tulips are
     jailyard blooms, they wear
d   [UNTITLED POEM] / (SEPT. 27, 1971), pp. xviii-xix: The
     ideogram
e   [UNTITLED POEM] / (OCT. 23, 1971), p. xix: the eye regards
     the
f   8 UNTITLED CHAPTERS, pp. 1-134
g   [UNTITLED PSALM], pp. 135-138: Blessed be the Lord the
     God of Israel who has
h   HARRISBURG: HOLY SATURDAY, APRIL 1, 1972, pp. 139-218

i ADDRESS BY FATHER DANIEL BERRIGAN, pp. 219-221
j APPENDIX (MESSAGE TO THE WEATHERMEN: EXCERPTS), pp. 222-227

A-22 PRISON POEMS. Greensboro, N.C.: Unicorn Press, 1973.

Poems. 124 pp. 23 cm. Dust jacket: black and white photograph of the author by Robert Fitch with black lettering on a white band. 3,000 cloth copies. Paperback edition published by Viking. (Some poems previously printed in *America Is Hard to Find* [in a different version].)

Contents:

a FOREWORD BY PHILIP BERRIGAN, pp. vii-viii
b THE PEARL OF GREAT PRICE, pp. 5-7: Variety of responses here!
c PATIENCE, HARD VIRTUE, pp. 8-9: Patience, tedious non Virtue
d A PRAYER TO THE BLESSED TRINITY, p. 10: I'm locked into the sins of General Motors
e WE USED TO MEET FOR CLASSES. SOMETIMES IT WAS ECSTASY, SOMETIMES BLAH, p. 11: The big claims of the powerless are not notably more
f IN PRISON, AS OUT, TIME IS OF THE ESSENCE, p. 12: Methodical rampage
g A SURVIVOR, p. 13: Youngest of trees, the ancient ginkgo,
h KERMIT, p. 14: 1 of those children of open spaces
i ALMOST EVERYBODY IS DYING HERE: ONLY A FEW ACTUALLY MAKE IT, p. 15: at 12:30 sharp
j I SAID NO NO, p. 16: i said: what you are doing
k HERE COMES ANOTHER REHABILITATED SPECIMEN: WATCH OUT, p. 17: home from v. nam
l SEEN ONE DAY FROM THE DENTAL CLINIC WINDOW, p. 18: Outside
m WE WERE PERMITTED TO MEET TOGETHER IN PRISON TO PREPARE FOR TRIAL, p. 19: yesterday, the usual stiff-necked shakedown
n GAMBLERS ANONYMOUS, p. 20: Odds are 400 to 1
o YOU COULD MAKE A SONG OF IT A DIRGE OF IT A HEART-BREAKER OF IT, p. 21: EVERYONE everyone in america
p O DANBURY, TO WHAT SHALL I COMPARE THEE?, p. 22: Like coming up against testy Charon in a bad time
q TULIPS IN THE PRISON YARD, pp. 23-24: Many poets, believe me, could do better by your

A-23 JESUS CHRIST. Garden City, N.Y.: Doubleday, 1973.

Meditations and poems. 24 August 1973. Unpaginated. 28 cm.
Dust jacket: red with blue and green design and white lettering by Gregory and Deborah Harris. 5,000 hardbound copies
and 10,000 paperback copies. (Illustrations by Gregory and
Deborah Harris.)

Contents:

a WAYS, pp. [8-9]: The hair-raising fanciful brutal quoti-
     dian ways
b [UNTITLED MEDITATIONS]: pp. [12-13], [16], [17], [20],
     [24], [25], [28-29, 32-33], [36-37], [40], [41, 44],
     [45], [56-57], [60-61], [64-65], [68], [69, 72], [73,
     76], [77], [88], [89], [96-97], [100-101], [104], [105],
     [108-109], [112-113, 116]
c THE CROSS AS MILITARY DECORATION, pp. [48-49]: The bust
     of a beribboned military man
d ON SALVATION OF SORTS, pp. [52-53]: Freak (origin un-
     known); one marked by physical deformity
e A READING (SORT OF) FROM PAUL'S 1ST LOVING LETTER / TO
     FRIENDS ON THE GREEK COAST (& TO US), pp. [80-81]:
     For those at the wheel of juggernaut, careening down-
     hill out of
f WHEN WE TALK TO YOU WHEN WE LISTEN TO YOU WHEN WE SAY,
     pp. [84-85]: no to you when we shut the front door and
     walk out and
g A MEDITATION FOR MADMEN, *OR HOW I WAS DRIVEN SANE BY THE
     REAL WORLD*, pp. [92-93]

A-24 SELECTED AND NEW POEMS. Garden City, N.Y.: Doubleday,
1973.

Poems. 7 September 1973. 293 pp. 22 cm. Dust jacket:
black and white photograph of author with orange and yellow
lettering. Cover typography by Judith Kazdym Leeds. Cover
photo by David Minor. 4,000 hardbound copies. 7,500 paperback copies. (Generous selections of previously collected
poems, some with slight changes by the author.)

Contents:

     I TIME WITHOUT NUMBER

a STARS ALMOST ESCAPE US, p. 3: They come unwilling
b BIRTHDAY IN QUEBEC / (eighty-six), pp. 4-5: I remember
     today a roadside, the crucifix

II ENCOUNTERS

eo   MY NAME, p. 191: If I were Pablo Neruda
ep   THE PILOTS, RELEASED, p. 192: When I think of you it is always (forgive me)
eq   THERE MUST BE A GOD, pp. 193–194: I thought I heard
er   THE CLOCK IN THE SQUARE REMINDS ME OF CERTAIN LIVES, p. 195: Ineffectuals
es   SOME SORT OF EXPLANATION, BETTER THAN NONE, p. 196: I cultivate a grin
et   SOMEHOW, p. 197: I kiss a book sometimes
eu   COME ALIVE (on the Long Island Railroad), p. 198: I had lost everything for a year
ev   SOMEWHERE THE EQUATION BREAKS DOWN, p. 199: between the perfect
ew   NOVEMBER 20, 1965, p. 200: Subway faces beheaded
ex   I WONDER, DO YOU, p. 201: know
ey   PEACEMAKING IS HARD / (*Jim and Sally*), p. 202: hard almost as war.
ez   THE TRIP, pp. 203–204: It was a foolish ricochet
fa   SEMINAR, p. 205: One speaker
fb   WALLS, p. 206: The wall
fc   A HARD DAY IN THE CITY, FOLLOWED BY FUN AND GAMES / (*for S.S.*), p. 207: One would have thought
fd   AN OLD WIFE REMEMBERS, p. 208: We started in a clapboard house that year
fe   1967--VIETNAM, p. 209: Two hands (fixation, horror)
ff   TRIP THROUGH MICHIGAN, p. 210: The poem started,
fg   TURNING THE PICTURE BOOK / (a Eucharistic procession), p. 211: Your unreal presence in a photo, passed
fh   A CIVIL RIGHTS DEMONSTRATION, p. 212: That morning I weighed
fi   ON THE TURNPIKE, p. 213: Who loaded history's pig iron
fj   BERGAMO: INSTRUCTIONS FOR GOING FORTH, p. 214: Alas if a man's death
fk   GUESS WHAT I ALMOST LOST TODAY, p. 215: A sidelong hairy look
fl   THE WEDDING / (*for David and Catherine Miller*), pp. 216–217: Make way, make way! the poor
fm   DIARY (Easter, 1966), pp. 218–219: I hadn't walked the tow path in Central Park
fn   JOHN ANDERSON MY JO JOHN, p. 220: Men cannot pluck or wear
fo   A SAINT ON THE DASHBOARD, p. 221: to hear. But not too near.
fp   A SEVERE CRITIC, A KIND OF ANSWER, p. 222: Of course, violence!
fq   SALVATION HISTORY, p. 223: I had a nightmare--
fr   WEST SIDE STORY, p. 224: A Broadway hash joint, a Puerto Rican

2. WADING AT SIX-MILE CREEK: LENT, BLOOD AND NO TEARS;
    1969, pp. 263-264: My favorite lower case
3. DEATH OF A DEER, pp. 265-266: Impaled
4. IN EXALTATION OF SO SIMPLE A THING, AN AUTUMN TREE,
    p. 267: Has not let blood
5. THE SERMON ON THE MOUNT, AND THE WAR THAT WILL NOT
    END FOREVER, p. 268: Jesus came down from Crough
    Patrick
6. 1879--MY FATHER--1969, p. 269: 90 bawling years, then
    you died off

ge *IN MEMORIAM; THOMAS MERTON*
1. 1969 OPENED LIKE THIS, p. 273: *I wish I had some joy--*
2. AT THE TIME OF HIS DEATH, AMERICANS HAD MASTERED THE
    DYNAMICS OF A MOON FLIGHT, p. 274: Merton's gone;
    that comfort ended.
3. EDIFYING ANECDOTES CONCERNING THE DECEASED ARE NOW IN
    ORDER, p. 275: January; a sick woman
4. MEMORIES AFTER THE FACT: A VISIT OF ILL-FAVORED
    CHARACTERS TO THE MONASTERY, p. 276: Under the
    stars, a last beer
5. WHO'S WHO AT THE OBSEQUIES, p. 277: General Hershey
    did not mourn
6. THE FUNERAL ORATION AS PRONOUNCED BY THE COMPASSION-
    ATE BUDDHA, pp. 278-280: Assembled sirs. The cour-
    tesies afforded us by the Dali Lama,

gf *FROM THE UNDERSIDE*
1. ANNOUNCEMENT, p. 281: Thursday a week, all weather
    forbidding
2. I WILL SIGN MY NAME, p. 282: Now what the hell sort
    of dog's life is left to limp?
3. QUESTION AND ANSWER, p. 283: Query: Shall a man then
    return
4. THE THREE GODS VISIT THE EARTH AND FIND IT WANTING,
    p. 284: I might be one of those gods in the old Zen
    tales or the testament,
5. THE DIVINE IDEA, p. 285: That divine idea Jesus cooked
    up in his Cordon Bleu intellect!
6. A PROFFER, p. 286: Look; a proffer slipped into the
    molars
7. RIVER, p. 287: My little friend a flutist sits far
    side of the river
8. WARNING, p. 288: Mind must learn to go like cat's or
    crow's feet
9. ON BEING HERE WITH PHIL / (5/29/71), pp. 289-291:
    Whenever I met a crook here
10. TULIPS IN THE PRISON YARD, pp. 292-293: All kinds of
    poets, believe me, could better praise your

A-25 VIETNAMESE LETTER. [Drawings by Tom Lewis.] New York: Hoa Binh Press, [1974?].

Poem. Date of publication not available. Unpaginated. 36 x 47 cm. No dust jacket. 250 signed copies; unknown number of copies printed. (Previously published in *Fellowship*, November 1973, as "A Letter to Vietnamese Prisoners." This version illustrated by Tom Lewis.)

Contents:

VIETNAMESE LETTER, [unpaginated]: Dear friends, your faces
    are a constriction of grief in the threat

A-26 LIGHTS ON IN THE HOUSE OF THE DEAD: A Prison Diary. Garden City, N.Y.: Doubleday, 1974.

Essays, meditations, and poems (diary). 15 March 1974. 309 pp. 22 cm. Dust jacket: gray with white, orange, and yellow lettering by Cheryl B. Asherman. Photograph of author on back by Barbara King. 5,000 hardbound copies. (Dedicated to Tom Buck and Bill Anderson.)

Contents:

a ACKNOWLEDGMENTS & DEDICATION, SORT OF, pp. 5-6
b NOTES ON SOCRATES: THE GODS OF THE STATE, pp. 7-8
c NEW GODS, pp. 9-20
d TO MARS, NOT TO US, pp. 21-28
e TALE OF A TALL ONE, pp. 29-33
f ["JUST TO SPITE THEM..."], pp. 35-41
g BORN WINNERS, BORN LOSERS, pp. 43-45
h NOTES FOR A STUDY GROUP; APT FOR IGNOMINY AND GLORY,
     pp. 47-64
i [THE WARDEN, THE LIEUTENANT, THE CAPTAIN, THE GUARD, THE
     SOCIAL], p. 62: The warden, the lieutenant, the captain,
     the guard, the social
j [IN THIS LUXURY HOUSING, HEATED TO A SWEATBOX, NIGHT AND
     DAY], p. 64: In this luxury housing, heated to a sweat-
     box, night and day
k LETTER TO J.C., pp. 65-75
l EVERY STRONG THOUGHT TURNS ME TO WATER, p. 74: Every
     strong thought turns me to water.
m THE INDICTMENTS COME DOWN, pp. 77-89
n YOU; SO NEAR NOT EXISTING, p. 87: You; so near not
     existing
o HOW MUCH TRUTH DO WE OWE THEM?, pp. 91-98

p   POP PRISON DESCRIBED, pp. 99-111
q   LETTER TO A CONGRESSMAN, pp. 113-120
r   WHAT TO DO WHEN THE SKY FALLS IN, pp. 121-131
s   LETTER TO THE CAMBRIDGE JESUITS, pp. 131-138
t   CATONSVILLE ON STAGE: THE WEIGHT OF AN ENDLESS AND POWER-
      LESS FOLLY, pp. 139-149
u   LETTER TO A HELLION, pp. 151-158
v   [MY FACE WHITE AS A POWDERED CLOWN'S], p. 157: My face
      white as a powdered clown's
w   FUN AND GAMES IN THE MOLAR FACTORY, pp. 159-173
x   WHAT CANNOT BE COUNTED CAN BE COUNTED ON, pp. 175-179
y   PORTRAIT OF A PRINCE OF HELL, pp. 181-193
z   HERE LIE THE GOOD GERMICANS, pp. 195-205
aa THE CHAIN: NOT AS SHORT AS IT HAS BEEN, NOT AS LONG AS IT
      WILL BE, pp. 207-222
ab THE LIGHT OF THE WORLD STRIKES IN VAIN: NO FIRE, pp. 223-
      227
ac AWAIT EVERYTHING, EXPECT NOTHING, pp. 229-236
ad WEEKEND VISIT, p. 229: They give a few of us a few minutes
      on the hill
ae MERTON: A BUDDHA WITH SWEAT ON HIS BROW, pp. 237-251
af A BIT OF A GO AT OUR MINISTER OF RELIGION, pp. 253-262
ag TONS OF TUNA, WALLEYED, NEAR TO TEARS, pp. 263-272
ah ATTICA, CHRONICLE, pp. 266-267: of cancerous inhibition;
ai THE UNDERSTANDING OF LIMITED GAINS, pp. 273-280
aj LOOK WHAT A MAN MIGHT BE, AND BE HEALED, pp. 281-288
ak BE IT HEREBY NOTED: ELEVEN PRISONERS TODAY BREAK BREAD
      ONCE MORE, pp. 289-298
al ANOTHER MOTHER FOR PEACE: A CHRISTMAS LETTER, pp. 299-306
am TO ROUND THIS OFF, A FEW RANDOM STORIES, pp. 307-309

A-27 THE RAFT IS NOT THE SHORE: Conversations Toward a Budd-
hist/Christian Awareness. Boston: Beacon, 1975. [Co-authored
by Thich Nhat Hanh.]

Conversations. 18 November 1975. 139 pp. 21 cm. Dust
jacket: white with black and red lettering by David Ford and
brown and black illustration by Vo-Dinh. Publication figures
not available. Paperback edition published by Beacon. (Woodcuts by Vo-Dinh.)

Contents:

a   1. MEMORY, EUCHARIST, DEATH, pp. 1-10
b   2. RELIGION IN THE WORLD, pp. 13-34
c   3. EXILE, pp. 37-47

d 4. PRIESTS AND PRISONERS, pp. 51-56
e 5. SELF-IMMOLATION, pp. 59-65
f 6. GOVERNMENT AND RELIGION, pp. 69-88
g 7. ECONOMICS AND RELIGION, pp. 91-103
h 8. JESUS AND BUDDHA, pp. 107-114
i 9. COMMUNITIES OF RESISTANCE, pp. 117-139

A-28 A BOOK OF PARABLES. New York: Seabury Press. A Cross-road Book, 1977.

Parables. 11 April 1977. 149 pp. 22 cm. Dust jacket: blue and orange lettering, green decoration with gold photograph on white background by unidentified designer. Publication figures not available. Published in hardbound edition only. (Dedicated to the author's mother, Frida Fromhart Berrigan.)

Contents:

a PREFACE, pp. ix-x
b EVE AND THE BIBLE SALESMAN, pp. 1-8
c THE PRISON LETTERS OF CAIN, pp. 9-20
d HOW NOAH MISSED THE BOAT, pp. 21-29
e THE TOWER OF BROTHERLY LOVE BLAH, BLAH, pp. 31-37
f THE FLEA IN PHAROAH'S EAR, pp. 39-47
g THE BODY COUNT OF KING DAVID, pp. 49-58
h THE WHALE'S TALE, pp. 59-67
i THE CURSE, pp. 69-77
j THE PATIENCE OF JOB IN DETROIT, MICHIGAN, pp. 79-89
k MOSES IN EGYPT: A DIARY OF EXILE, pp. 91-93
l WINNERS/LOSERS OR WHOSE GOD IS FOR REAL, pp. 95-100
m THE TENTH GENERATION ACCORDING TO DANIEL, pp. 101-110
n THE BOOK OF ABDIAH: A COMMENTARY OF SORTS, pp. 111-115
o A BRIEF PRESS CONFERENCE WITH GOD ON THE FATE OF A FAVOR-
     ITE SON, p. 117
p JEREMIAH, OR GOD IS A DOWNER, pp. 119-123
q THE FIORETTI OF SAINT ELISEUS, pp. 125-149

A-29 UNCOMMON PRAYER: A Book of Psalms. New York: Seabury Press. A Crossroad Book. 1978.

Poems and essays. 27 March 1978. 145 pp. 22 cm. Dust jacket: blue, white, and brown lettering on black background by Barbara Hall with blue woodcut by Robert McGovern. Publication figures not available. Published in hardbound edition only.

A-29: dust jacket by Robert McGovern

(Excerpts published in the *Catholic Worker* and the *Other Side*. Dedicated to Jonah House members. Woodcuts by Robert McGovern.)

Contents:

A-30 BESIDE THE SEA OF GLASS: The Song of the Lamb. New
York: Seabury Press, 1978.

Meditations and poem. 25 September 1978. 110 pp. 22½ cm.
Cover photograph by Frank Kostyu. Publication figures not
available. Published in paperback edition only. (Photographs
by Frank Kostyu.)

Contents:

a   INTRODUCTION, pp. 9-15
b   HOW THE SEA GREW CALM AS GLASS, AND WHEN AND WHY, pp. 17-
      33
c   BY THE SEA OF GLASS: THE PRAYER OF THE LAMB, pp. 35-110
d   [WITH REGARD TO THE GREAT YOU], pp. 101-103: with regard
      to the great You

A-31 THE WORDS OUR SAVIOR GAVE US. Springfield, Ill.: Temple-
gate Publishers, 1978.

Meditations. 15 October 1978. 123 pp. 21⅓ cm. Publication figures not available. Published in paperback edition
only.

Contents:

a   OUR FATHER, pp. 11-29
b   YOU WHO ARE IN HEAVEN, pp. 31-43
c   HALLOWED BE YOUR NAME, pp. 45-56
d   YOUR KINGDOM COME, pp. 59-70
e   YOUR WILL BE DONE ON EARTH AS IT IS IN HEAVEN, pp. 73-81
f   GIVE US THIS DAY OUR DAILY BREAD, pp. 83-94
g   FORGIVE THE WRONGS WE HAVE COMMITTED, AS WE FORGIVE THE
      WRONGS WE HAVE DONE TO OTHERS, pp. 97-108
h   AND LEAD US NOT INTO TEMPTATION, BUT DELIVER US FROM
      EVIL, pp. 111-118
i   AN AFTERWORD, pp. 121-123

B

DANIEL BERRIGAN
Contributions to Books by Other Authors

1963

B-1   THE SPIRIT OF MODERN SACRED ART in William J. Leonard,
       S.J. (editor). *Liturgy for the People: Essays in Honor
       of Gerald Ellard, S.J.* Milwaukee: Bruce, 1963. Pp.
       147-167.

1967

B-2   FOREWORD in [Sister] Mary Corita [Kent]. *Footnotes
       and Headlines: A Play - Pray Book.* New York: Herder
       and Herder, 1967. Unpaginated.

       This piece, written in free verse, is subtitled FOOT-
       NOTES, FANCY FREE and it begins: The worst thing is an
       omnivorous solemnity.

B-3   [INTERVIEW WITH JAMES FINN] in James Finn (editor).
       Protest: Pacifism and Politics. New York: Random
       House, 1967. Pp. 141-153.

1968

B-4   DIARY FROM THE UNDERGROUND in Malcolm Boyd (editor).
       The Underground Church. New York: Sheed and Ward,
       1968. Pp. 50-62.

B-5   FOREWORD in Christopher William Jones. *Listen Pilgrim.*
       Milwaukee: Bruce Publishing, 1968. Pp. vii-x.

B-6   THE MODERN CONCEPT OF "MISSIO" in Raymond A. Schroth,
       S.J., et al. *Jesuit Spirit in a Time of Change.* West-
       minster, Md.: Newman Press, 1968. Pp. 203-220.

                              1969

B-7   FOREWORD in David Kirk (compiler and editor). *Quota-*
       tions from Chairman Jesus. Springfield, Ill.: Temple-
       gate, 1969. Pp. ix-xiii.

       The verse begins: The gospel of Jesus is spoken in a
       world.

B-8   FOREWORD in Jean-Marie Paupert. *The Politics of the*
       Gospel. Translated by Gregor Roy. New York: Holt,
       Rinehart and Winston, 1969. Pp. vi-xviii.

                              1970

B-9   THE BREAKING OF MEN AND THE BREAKING OF BREAD: AN INTRO-
       DUCTION in Philip Berrigan. *Prison Journals of a*
       Priest Revolutionary. Edited by Vincent McGee. New
       York: Holt, Rinehart and Winston, 1970. Pp. xi-xix.

                              1971

B-10   INTRODUCTION in Bob [Robert Beck] Fitch. *My Eyes*
       Have Seen. San Francisco: Glide Publications, 1971.
       P. [i].

B-11   LET'S SAY *NO* IF IT NEEDS SAYING in George Riemer (edi-
       tor). *The New Jesuits.* Boston: Little, Brown, 1971.
       Pp. 34-64.

B-12   LETTER TO THE WEATHERMEN in William Van Etten Casey,
       S.J., and Philip Nobile (editors). *The Berrigans.*
       New York: Avon Books, 1971. Pp. 203-213.

B-13 PREFACE. A HOMILY BY A FUGITIVE PRIEST in William
      Stringfellow and Anthony Towne. *Suspect Tenderness:*
      The Ethics of the Berrigan Witness. New York: Holt,
      Rinehart and Winston, 1971. Pp. 3-10.

      Opposite the title page, the poem MAN IS MORE is
      reprinted.

                              1972

B-14 A FOOL'S CALLING (January 1, 1972) in Dorothy Day. *On*
      Pilgrimage: The Sixties. New York: Curtis Books, 1972.
      P. 5.

      The poem, dedicated to Dorothy Day, begins: I put to
      myself a fool's calling.

B-15 EPILOGUE in Stephen Halpert and Tom Murray (editors).
      Witness of the Berrigans. Garden City, N.Y.: Doubleday,
      1972. Pp. 199-200.

B-16 INTRODUCTION in Horst Bienek. *The Cell*. Translated by
      Ursula Mahlendorf. Santa Barbara, Calif.: Unicorn
      Press, 1972. Pp. i-v.

      Includes untitled poem on p. v that begins: I put to
      myself a fool's calling.

B-17 SERMON FROM THE UNDERGROUND, AUGUST 2, 1970 in Stephen
      Halpert and Tom Murray (editors). *Witness of the Ber-*
      rigans. Garden City, N.Y.: Doubleday, 1972. Pp. 140-
      143.

B-18 "...THEIR SPEECH IS ALL OF FORGIVENESS..." (foreword)
      in Thich Nhat Hanh. *The Path of Return Continues the*
      Journey. [New York?]: Hoa Binh Press, [1972?]. Pp.
      3-4.

                              1973

B-19 THE EUCHARIST AND SURVIVAL (discussion with Daniel Ber-
      rigan) in Alistair Kee (editor). *Seeds of Liberation:*
      Spiritual Dimensions to Political Struggle. London: SCM
      [Student Christian Movement] Press, 1973. Pp. 72-80.

B-20 THE MARK OF THE BEAST in Alistair Kee (editor). *Seeds of Liberation: Spiritual Dimensions to Political Struggle*. London: SCM [Student Christian Movement] Press, 1973. Pp. 7-15.

B-21 PROPERTY (discussion with Daniel Berrigan) in Alistair Kee (editor). *Seeds of Liberation: Spiritual Dimensions to Political Struggle*. London: SCM [Student Christian Movement] Press, 1973. Pp. 68-71.

B-22 PSALM FOR TWO VOICES (For Elizabeth McAlister) in Philip Berrigan. *Widen the Prison Gates: Writing from Jails, April 1970-December 1972*. New York: Simon & Schuster, 1973. Pp. [11-12].

The poem begins: Dry stones we bruise we are bruised.

B-23 SANITY IN FACE OF THE BEAST in Alistair Kee (editor). *Seeds of Liberation: Spiritual Dimensions to Political Struggle*. London: SCM [Student Christian Movement] Press, 1973. Pp. 37-42.

B-24 WHERE IS COMMUNITY? (discussion with Daniel Berrigan) in Alistair Kee (editor). *Seeds of Liberation: Spiritual Dimensions to Political Struggle*. London: SCM [Student Christian Movement] Press, 1973. Pp. 45-54.

1974

B-25 INTRODUCTION in Bo Wirmark. *The Buddhists in Vietnam: An Alternative View of the War*. Edited by Joseph Gerson. Brussels: War Resisters' International, 1974. Pp. 1-5.

B-26 THE MIDDLE EAST: SANE CONDUCT in *The Great Berrigan Debate* (no editor cited). New York: Committee on New Alternatives in the Middle East, 1974. Pp. 1-8.

B-27 SANE CONDUCT?...A DEBATE in *The Great Berrigan Debate* (with Hans Morgenthau) (no editor cited). New York: Committee on New Alternatives in the Middle East, 1974. Pp. 21-26.

1975

B-28   FOREWORD in Chuck Sullivan. *Vanishing Species: Poems*.
       Charlotte, N.C.: Red Clay Books, 1975. Pp. [5-6].

C

DANIEL BERRIGAN
Contributions to Periodicals

1942

C-1   STORM SONG
       America 67, 13 June 1942, p. 271.
       Lady, the Maytime mirrors you very well--

1943

C-2   YOU VESTED US THIS MORNING (for four soldier-brothers)
       America 70, 23 October 1943, p. 75.
       You vested us this morning

1944

C-3   FAITH AND POETRY
       America 70, 1 January 1944, pp. 353-354.

C-4   FORGOTTEN SPLENDOR
       America 70, 4 March 1944, pp. 605-606.

1946

C-5   TO SPRING, A CHILD
       America 75, 3 August 1946, p. 418.
       Winter like a dust of snow

C-6   ABELARD
       Spirit 13, September 1946, p. 115.
       Though very small my heart,

C-7   THE MOTHER
       America 76, 21 December 1946, p. 327.
       Not amid faces intense, fulfilled, adoring,

                              1947

C-8   THE MARTYRS' LAST HOUR
       Ye Domesday Booke [Georgetown University], 1947, p. 24.
       While yet this pitiful hour remains, we stand

C-9   LEVITE
       America 76, 15 February 1947, p. 550.
       With a thoughtful spider to lace the window

C-10   PIPER
       Spirit 14, July 1947, pp. 70-71.
       What fool is born

                              1948

C-11   FAILURE
       Atlantic Monthly 181, May 1948, p. 107.
       I am mindful of failure that crowns the unborn

C-12   LIVING I SHALL LIVE
       Spirit 15, July 1948, pp. 74-75.
       No more austere, no more possessed he is

C-13   THE CHRISTENING: FOR BRIGID
       Spirit 15, September 1948, pp. 104-105.
       Love taking thought

                              1949

C-14   TWENTY-SEVEN
       Spirit 15, January 1949, p. 175.
       The years have dried: their waters

C-15   THE AUNT
       Spirit 16, May 1949, p. 51.
       With eyes a dying candle

C-16   THE COAT
       Spirit 16, July 1949, p. 75.
       This is the coat His bowed mother fitted

C-17   MY BROTHER PRONOUNCES HIS VOWS
       Spirit 16, September 1949, pp. 116-117.
       My mind had sought

1950

C-18   THE SWORD AND THE BALANCE
       Modern Humanist [Weston, Mass.] 6, May 1950, pp. 2-8.

C-19   [EDITORIAL]
       Modern Humanist [Weston, Mass.] 7, October 1950, pp. 2-3.

C-20   JUBILEE CHANT (for Fathers Keyes and Brock)
       Modern Humanist [Weston, Mass.] 7, October 1950, p. 4.
       I am renewed to rising by that Sun.

C-21   JUBILEE CHANT
       Spirit 17, November 1950, p. 139.
       I am renewed to rising by that sun

C-22   A NOTE ON THE MARTYRS OF KOREA
       Modern Humanist [Weston, Mass.] 7, December 1950, pp. 19-21.

1951

C-23   THE SEED (In Peace: SML)
       Modern Humanist [Weston, Mass.] 8, Autumn, 1951, pp.
       [iv-v].
       Unless the seed, He said....

C-24   THE NEW POETRY: DEFINITION, SOURCES, AND AN EXAMPLE
       Modern Humanist [Weston, Mass.] 8, Autumn 1951, pp. 1-14.

C-25   MY LOVE SPOKE FOR ME (for Philip, on His Profession)
       Spirit 18, September 1951, pp. 104-105.
       In the grave Lenten time

1952

C-26   THE SEED (In Peace: S.M.L.)
        Spirit 18, January 1952, pp. 166-168.
        Unless the seed, He said....

C-27   PROEM
        Spirit 19, March 1952, p. 13.
        I sing the star whose light

C-28   THE POET TO HIMSELF
        Spirit 19, May 1952, p. 38.
        Color it not kind

C-29   SONNET TO THE BOY
        Spirit 19, July 1952, p. 76.
        He too, He too shook vainly as a flower

1953

C-30   ISRAEL, THE CHURCH, AND HISTORY
        Modern Humanist [Weston, Mass.] 9, Winter 1953, pp.
            27-47.

C-31   FOR AN ETERNAL REMEMBRANCE: JUNE 21, 1952
        Spirit 19, January 1953, pp. 167-169.
        Winter is hard: it reminds us how that mother,

C-32   LITTLE HOURS FOR OUR LADY
        Spirit 20, September 1953, pp. 112-113.
        So when she held Him close in the firelight, her
            adoration

1954

C-33   LET US MAKE TO OUR IMAGE
        Spirit 21, November 1954, p. 139.
        When the word struck, it was all fountains

C-34   THE WORKMEN
        Month [London] N.S. 12, December 1954, p. 347.
        This is the body the seasons sold for money,

1955

C-35   THAT TOTAL CHILDHOOD
           Spirit 21, January 1955, p. 167.
           Some young god had taken this spell on himself

C-36   THE INNOCENT THRONE (for the Ordination of my brother;
               June 1955)
           Spirit 22, May 1955, p. 48.
           My laced and living memories arise

1956

C-37   LONELINESS
           Spirit 22, January 1956, p. 167.
           To be a part of things, to be apart from them;

C-38   FINALITY
           Spirit 23, May 1956, p. 38.
           Trees say in a moment what they have in mind.

C-39   PENTECOST
           Spirit 23, May 1956, p. 39.
           All their lives rounded in a backcountry brogue:

C-40   STARS ALMOST ESCAPE US
           Spirit 23, May 1956, p. 39.
           Stars almost escape us. They come unwilling

1957

C-41   BELIEVE
           Thought 32, Summer 1957, p. 259.
           That delicate honeycomb Christ took to mouth,

C-42   CREDENTIALS
           Thought 32, Summer 1957, p. 256.
           I would it were possible to state in so

C-43   FIVE POEMS
           Thought 32, Summer 1957, pp. 255-259.

See separate listings for: MOON, CREDENTIALS, SAYS
   GOD, THE MEN ON THE HILL, BELIEVE.

C-44   THE MEN ON THE HILL
       Thought 32, Summer 1957, p. 258.
       There is still time to escape

C-45   MOON
       Thought 32, Summer 1957, p. 255.
       This desolate cold god

C-46   SAYS GOD
       Thought 32, Summer 1957, p. 256.
       I would even give my Son to them

C-47   [REVIEW OF *THE BIBLE AND THE LITURGY* BY JEAN DANIÉLOU]
       Thought 32, Winter 1957, pp. 622-623.

C-48   STARS ALMOST ESCAPE US
       Saturday Review 15, 20 July 1957, p. 40.
       They come unwilling

C-49   DOMES
       America 98, 19 October 1957, p. 72.
       that raise the improbable to an art,

C-50   FLOWERS
       America 98, 26 October 1957, p. 111.
       Comparing them to the sea

C-51   LANDSCAPES THERE ARE
       America 98, 26 October 1957, p. 111.
       of such formal will

C-52   EACH DAY WRITES
       New York *Times Book Review*, 10 November 1957,
          p. 2.
       In my heart's core

C-53   OUR VERY HEART
       New York *Times Book Review*, 10 November 1957,
          p. 2.
       The leaves are fallen, the birds

1958

C-54 TREES INSIST ON THE MIND:
      Espirit [University of Scranton] 1, Spring 1958, p. 1.
      compression of life

C-55 BEETHOVEN'S VIOLIN (for Carol and Jerry)
      Chelsea Review number 1, Summer 1958, pp. 15-16.
      Birnam wood across the plain, marches

C-56 CATHOLICITY AND ITS MEN
      Catholic Library Association Proceedings 34, March 1958,
         pp. 31-34.

C-57 PHILOMELA
      Spirit 25, March 1958, pp. 16-17.
      That it should dare

C-58 RESPONSIBILITY AND THE WORD
      Spirit 25, March 1958, pp. 21-23.

      Address before Catholic Poetry Society on 30 January
      1958.

C-59 SOUL TO BODY
      Spirit 25, March 1958, p. 17.
      Substance of things

C-60 MORE LIKE THE SEA
      Poetry 92, August 1958, p. 301.
      Nail him to sticks

C-61 [REVIEW OF *DOCTOR RABELAIS*, BY D.B. WYNDHAM LEWIS]
      Thought 33, August 1958, pp. 449-450.

C-62 JOB IN SUBURBIA
      America 100, 4 October 1958, pp. 12-13.

C-63 LIFE IS PERPETUAL ADVENT, A DAILY CALL TO ACTION
      Catholic Messenger, 27 November 1958, p. 1.

C-64 JOHN WAS NOT THE LIGHT, HE POINTED TO IT; SO MUST WE
      Catholic Messenger, 4 December 1958, p. 1.

C-65 THE ONE WHOM YOU DO NOT KNOW--A RIDDLE FOR ADVENT
      Catholic Messenger, 11 December 1958, p. 1.

C-66   WE STAND AT CHRISTMAS, WE STAND AT THE END OF THINGS
       Catholic Messenger, 18 December 1958, p. 1.

                              1959

C-67   EVE
       Chelsea Review number 4, Spring 1959, p. 22.
       It was for love of me

C-68   EVE
       Thought 34, Spring 1959, p. 54.
       An old woman of hearth and field,

C-69   FIVE ENCOUNTERS
       Thought 34, Spring 1959, pp. 54-56.

       See separate listings for EVE, JOSEPH, SAINT ANNE,
       LAZARUS, MAGDALEN.

C-70   JOSEPH
       Thought 34, Spring 1959, p. 54.
       One corner of south field my plow veered from

C-71   LAZARUS
       Thought 34, Spring 1959, p. 55.
       After my universe was only

C-72   MAGDALEN
       Thought 34, Spring 1959, p. 56.
       Two pebbles on water make marriage rings:

C-73   MAN IS MORE
       Chelsea Review number 4, Spring 1959, pp. 23-24.
       than the face of his father

C-74   SAINT ANNE / (who bore a child in late life)
       Thought 34, Spring 1959, p. 55.
       Hand that folded and laid aside my fabric

C-75   TREE: OCTOBER
       Chelsea Review number 4, Spring 1959, p. 24.
       Under that autumn cloud

C-76   THE HOLY MOTHER AT TWILIGHT
       Marianist 50, January 1959, p. 7.
       Birds and lambs bound

C-77 [REVIEW OF *HOLY PAGANS OF THE OLD TESTAMENT*, BY JEAN
       DANIÉLOU, S.J.]
       Worship 33, January 1959, pp. 96-99.

C-78 THIS ORDER OF SMALL CONSEQUENCE
       Spirit 25, January 1959, p. 165.
       This order of small consequence

C-79 ABRAHAM
       Commonweal 69, 16 January 1959, p. 405.
       To see my small son

C-80 IN A RACE, ONE WINS / (The Point of Lent)
       Ave Maria 89, 7 February 1959, pp. 10-11.

       1st in series: The Point of Lent.

C-81 TOTAL RECALL / (The Point of Lent)
       Ave Maria 89, 14 February 1959, pp. 10-11.

       2nd in series: The Point of Lent.

C-82 THE GREATEST OF THESE / (The Point of Lent)
       Ave Maria 89, 21 February 1959, pp. 10-11.

       3rd in series: The Point of Lent.

C-83 ASHES AND RESURRECTION / (The Point of Lent)
       Ave Maria 89, 28 February 1959, pp. 20-21.

       4th in series: The Point of Lent.

C-84 ALL THINGS IN PLACE / (The Point of Lent)
       Ave Maria 89, 7 March 1959, pp. 8-9.

       5th in series: The Point of Lent.

C-85 PARABLES AND SIGNS / (The Point of Lent)
       Ave Maria 89, 14 March 1959, pp. 24-25.

       6th in series: The Point of Lent.

C-86 UNTO THE END: A MEDITATION / (The Point of Lent)
       Ave Maria 89, 21 March 1959, pp. 9, 23.

       7th in series: The Point of Lent.

C-87 I AM STILL WITH YOU / (The Point of Lent)
       Ave Maria 89, 28 March 1959, pp. 25-26.

       Final in series: The Point of Lent.

C-88   I SING MEMORY
       Spirit 26, May 1959, p. 40.
       I sing memory that clothes

C-89   SAINT JOHN BAPTIST
       Spirit 26, May 1959, pp. 39-40.
       A sword forbade me to grow old: it cut

C-90   TREE
       Spirit 26, May 1959, p. 40.
       Unlike a fish that gestures feebly

C-91   DEATH
       Poetry 94, July 1959, p. 231.
       We look in friend's eyes:

C-92   ELEGY
       Poetry 94, July 1959, p. 232.
       Permanent beauty stands

C-93   PARABLE
       Poetry 94, July 1959, p. 233.
       Hemlocks in row, heads bowed beneath snowfall

C-94   SAINT JOHN BAPTIST
       Poetry 94, July 1959, p. 231.
       In the mirror a sword made descending

C-95   SNOWMAN
       Poetry 94, July 1959, p. 232.
       The children wrapped up and skeined out and

C-96   CHRISTIAN HUMANISM
       Catholic Messenger, 27 August 1959, p. 6.

C-97   A STATUE OF THE BLESSED VIRGIN, CARVED IN WOOD
       Sponsa Regis 31, December 1959, p. 106.
       Wood is noble when it forgets to resemble

C-98   LONELINESS (Saint Joseph)
       Commonweal 71, 11 December 1959, p. 317.
       Vexing the the heart, old scenes returned:

1960

C-99   THE SPIRITS THAT SPEAK IN US (to my brother Philip)
       Thought 35, Summer 1960, pp. 247-250.
       --What shall we form to him: Lord Hell's mask

C-100 THE PROPHETIC SPIRIT OF THE LAYMAN
       Grail Review 2, 4th Quarter 1960, pp. 4-7.

C-101 SAINT STEPHEN
       Commonweal 71, 1 January 1960, p. 390.
       That day stones fell

C-102 LAZARUS
       Spirit 27, May 1960, p. 39.
       Silence rolled over and over my body its

C-103 MARY
       Spirit 27, May 1960, pp. 38-39.
       A maiden's untroubled speech

C-104 SAINT JOSEPH
       Spirit 27, May 1960, p. 39.
       What draws heart and

C-105 THAT DREAM, THAT TOTAL CHILDHOOD: AN ESSAY ON CHILD-
           HOOD IN PHOTOGRAPHS AND POETRY
       Sign 40, August 1960, pp. 44-49.

       Photographs by Jacques Lowe.

C-106 SACRIFICE AND MODERN MAN
       Sponsa Regis 32, November 1960, pp. 72-83.

C-107 THOUGHTS OF A FORTIETH YEAR?
       Commonweal 73, 4 November 1960, p. 150.
       Nothing so portentous, But I recall

C-108 TERESA OF AVILA
       Commonweal 73, 30 December 1960, p. 364.
       Almighty God could make again

1961

C-109   BLIND MAN
        Poetry 97, March 1961, p. 364.
        Drawn that stand like chevaliers to man

C-110   CRY
        Poetry 97, March 1961, p. 364.
        Contain me, cried stag's nostril and eye

C-111   GREAT GOD PAUSED AMONG MEN
        Poetry 97, March 1961, p. 363.
        and spoke: *coopers, craftsmen, shepherds*

C-112   SAINT MATTHEW, PUBLICAN
        Poetry 97, March 1961, p. 363.
        The face upon Caesar's coin

C-113   A STATUE OF THE BLESSED VIRGIN, CARVED IN IVORY
        Poetry 97, March 1961, p. 365.
        The herd of time riding, an intellectual

C-114   MY LADY MARY
        Spirit 28, May 1961, pp. 41-42.
        Did journeyman phrases

C-115   NOT YET
        Spirit 28, May 1961, p. 41.
        I remember this;

C-116   SUN
        Spirit 28, May 1961, p. 40.
        We run toward flesh

C-117   WINTER UPON OUR EYES
        Spirit 28, May 1961, p. 40.
        do the dead endure, eyeless and stern

C-118   THE CATHOLIC DREAM WORLD AND THE SACRED IMAGE
        Worship 35, September 1961, pp. 549-560.

C-119   THE EFFORT OF UNDERSTANDING
        Spirit 28, November 1961, p. 117.
        Look up

C-120   SAINT PETER REMEMBERS
        Spirit 28, November 1961, pp. 121-122.
        His guise

C-121 STATUE OF THE BLESSED VIRGIN CARVED IN WOOD
       Commonweal 75, 29 December 1961, p. 356.
       Truly love wishes

                              1962

C-122 THE ETERNAL YOUTH OF THE CHURCH
       North American Liturgical Week 23, 1962, pp. 1-15.

C-123 THE SPRINGS OF SILENCE
       Thought 37, Spring 1962, pp. 74-92.

       A play based on the life of Charles de Foucauld, and
       broadcast on the ABC television network, 27 November
       1960.

C-124 EYES OF MAN
       American Scholar 31, Summer 1962, p. 431.
       not Promethean, not a wall's holy image, conceding

C-125 TREE
       American Scholar 31, Summer 1962, p. 431.
       It takes measure of man

C-126 AUTHENTICALLY CHRISTIAN ART
       Theology Digest 10, Fall 1962, pp. 207-208.

C-127 SACRAMENTS ARE ON BEHALF OF MAN
       Commonweal 75, 16 March 1962, p. 643.
       The people, men and women together

C-128 PHOTO
       Commonweal 76, 6 April 1962, p. 35.
       My grandmother, by time diminished

C-129 SAINT JOSEPH SPEAKS (in memoriam: Ed Willock)
       Spirit 29, May 1962, pp. 39-41.
       Because I am near to you and yet not near

C-130 THE NEW SPIRIT OF MODERN SACRED ART
       Critic 20, July 1962, pp. 30-33.

C-131 IN MEMORIAM
       Poetry 100, August 1962, p. 285.
       A magisterial touch was firm

C-132   IRONIES
        Poetry 100, August 1962, p. 285.
        What moves me are ironies

C-133   THE LENS
        Poetry 100, August 1962, p. 283.
        Poignant, this counterpoint

C-134   MORTALITY
        Poetry 100, August 1962, p. 284.
        A leaf's falling tells

C-135   [A WONDER OF ORIGINS]
        Poetry 100, August 1962, p. 284.
        A wonder of origins; flower points to a bird,

C-136   THE CHRISTIAN AND HIS TIMES
        Perspectives 7, November-December 1962, pp. 159-163.

C-137   THE FACE OF CHRIST
        Ave Maria 96, 15 December 1962, p. 22.
        The tragic beauty of the face of Christ

C-138   LANDSCAPES THERE ARE
        Ave Maria 96, 15 December 1962, p. 22.
        Landscapes there are of such formal will and silken
            atmosphere

C-139   TWO POEMS
        Ave Maria 96, 15 December 1962, p. 22.

        See separate listings for THE FACE OF CHRIST and
        LANDSCAPES THERE ARE.

C-140   MIDWINTER
        Ave Maria 96, 22 December 1962, p. 10.
        Unmoving light,

C-141   A STATUE OF THE BLESSED VIRGIN, CARVEN IN WOOD
        Ave Maria 96, 22 December 1962. p. 10.
        Truly love wishes

C-142   NATIVITY
        Syracuse *Post-Standard* [*Pictorial*], 23 December 1962,
            p. 5.
        Prodigious Caesar rakes the village clean

1963

C-143   ARCHBISHOP ROBERTS INTERVIEWED IN LONDON ON WAR
            MORALITY
        Unity, 1963, pp. 1-4.

        Published under the pseudonym "John Paulson."

C-144   COMPASSION
        Continuum 1, Summer 1963, p. 259.
        I could sing statuary

C-145   I FEAR MOST, I THINK
        Continuum 1, Summer 1963, p. 260.
        if nightmare is oracle, or that ambition

C-146   MAN IS AN ABYSS, AUGUSTINE CRIED
        Continuum 1, Summer 1963, p. 258.
        I saw wild hate and wilder love

C-147   POSTSCRIPT TO THE MARCH ON WASHINGTON
        Continuum 1, Autumn 1963, pp. 406-408.

        Co-authored with Philip Berrigan.

C-148   MODERN TRENDS PROD CATHOLICS TO "SHAPE UP"
        World Campus 6, January 1963, pp. 1-2.

C-149   REFLECTIONS ON THE CHURCH [I]
        Today 18, January 1963, pp. 16-20.

        Art by Margaret Dagenais.

C-150   THE SACRAMENTS ARE ON BEHALF OF MAN
        Ave Maria 96, 12 January 1963, p. 27.
        The people, men and women together

C-151   NEW MEN IN THE MAKING [Reflections on the Church II]
        Today 18, February 1963, pp. 14-17.

        Art by Margaret Dagenais.

C-152   ASTONISHMENT
        Today 18, May 1963, p. 13.
        And wonder why the cancer reconvenes

C-153   CHRIST AND THE SHAPE OF MANKIND
        Catholic Worker, May 1963, pp. 2, 7, 8.

        Co-authored with Philip Berrigan.

C-154 RACIAL MARCH MOVING EXPERIENCE
       Syracuse *Post-Standard*, 8 September 1963, p. 6.

       Co-authored with Philip Berrigan.

C-155 THE ETERNAL YOUTH OF THE CHURCH
       Catholic Messenger, 12 September 1963, p. 5.

       Excerpts from a talk at 1962 North American Liturgical
       Week.

C-156 ARCHBISHOP ROBERTS: THE COUNCIL AND PEACE
       Catholic Worker, October 1963, pp. 2, 7.

       Published under the pseudonym "John Paulson."

C-157 ARCHBISHOP ROBERTS AND THE PEACE QUESTION
       Catholic Worker, November 1963, pp. 2, 6, 7.

       Published under the pseudonym "Jonas Winters."

C-158 IF
       Spirit 34, November 1963, p. 132.
       If I am not built up

C-159 TALISMAN
       Spirit 34, November 1963, p. 133.
       I wear

C-160 YOU TOO, BY THE SEA
       Spirit 34, November 1963, p. 130.
       Life; a vast knot of stinking

C-161 COME FEED THE WORLD
       Commonweal 79, 8 November 1963, p. 187.
       Is the world then, more

C-162 A PITTSBURGH BEGGAR REMINDS ME OF THE DEAD OF HIROSHIMA
       Today 19, December 1963, pp. 18-19.
       Seeing the beggar's sign

                              1964

C-163 LINES
       Continuum 2, Spring 1964, p. 123.
       A peace treaty signed

C-164 A YOUNG BIRD FOUND DYING, BROUGHT INDOORS
       Continuum 2, Spring 1964, p. 122.
       The moral of this

C-165   *AMERICA* AND THE RED TERROR
        Continuum 1, Winter 1964, pp. 581-583.

C-166   THE BOOK
        Thought 39, Winter 1964, pp. 585-586.
        A living eye rested on the book,

C-167   IRONIES
        Thought 39, Winter 1964, pp. 588-589.
        Time's white maned river

C-168   LAST DAY
        Thought 39, Winter 1964, pp. 586-587.
        When He did come, all the

C-169   THE POEM
        Thought 39, Winter 1964, p. 588.
        When I see flowers borne into a city room

C-170   PRAGUE: OLD WOMAN IN THE STREET
        Thought 39, Winter 1964, p. 585.
        In the country saying, she was only

C-171   RACISM AND ROMAN CATHOLICS
        Continuum 1, Winter 1964, pp. 516-522.

        Co-authored with Philip Berrigan.

C-172   SEVEN POEMS
        Thought 39, Winter 1964, pp. 585-589.

        See individual listings for PRAGUE: OLD WOMAN IN THE
        STREET, THE BOOK, SONG (from Jacopone da Todi), LAST
        DAY, SORROW, THE POEM, IRONIES.

C-173   SONG (from Jacopone da Todi)
        Thought 39, Winter 1964, p. 586.
        In my morning prayer

C-174   SORROW
        Thought 39, Winter 1964, p. 587.
        I saw a mother mourning her sick child

C-175   CHRISTIANS WITHIN MARXISM
        Unity, January 1964, p. 1.

C-176   EXPLORING OUR FREEDOM [I]
        Today 19, January 1964, pp. 12-15.

        Art by Petrie Joan Bertolis.

C-177   AIR TRIP TO BOSTON
        Today 19, February 1964, p. 15.
        I may become

C-178   CATECHUMEN
        Today 19, February 1964, p. 15.
        Christ's prophetic soul

C-179   THE MODERN CONCEPT OF "MISSIO"
        Woodstock Letters 93, February 1964, pp. 11-30.

C-180   NEW CHRISTIANS WORK WITHIN NEW MARXISM
        Unity, February 1964, pp. 1-3.

C-181   THREE POEMS
        Today 19, February 1964, p. 15.

        See separate listings for AIR TRIP TO BOSTON, CATECHU-
        MEN, THE WRITING OF A POEM.

C-182   THE WRITING OF A POEM
        Today 19, February 1964, p. 15.
        The greatness of art

C-183   THE LITURGICAL ARTS
        Critic 22, February-March 1964, pp. 59-60.

C-184   [LETTER TO DOROTHY DAY]
        Catholic Worker, March 1964, p. 5.

        Published under the pseudonym "John Paulson."

C-185   THE SPIRIT OF YOUTH [I]
        Queen's Work 56, March 1964, pp. 16-19.

C-186   THE COUNCIL AND THE PRIEST
        Perspectives 9, March-April 1964, pp. 52-55.

        Published under the pseudonym "John Winter."

C-187   A DARK WORD
        Poetry 104, April 1964, p. 13.
        As I walk patiently through life

C-188   THE FACE OF SOUTH AFRICA: 10 MILLION AT MERCY OF
           WHITE
        Unity, April 1964, pp. 1-3.

        Published under the pseudonym "John Paulson."

C-189 HENRY MOORE IN THE GARDEN
Poetry 104, April 1964, p. 12.
The hard wrought face

C-190 THE SPIRIT OF YOUTH [II]
Queen's Work 56, April 1964, pp. 16-20.

C-191 THE "UNPROTECTED" LIFE [EXPLORING OUR FREEDOM II]
Today 19, April 1964, pp. 12-14.

Art by Petrie Joan Bertolis.

C-192 WE ARE IN LOVE, THE CELIBATES GRAVELY SAY
Poetry 104, April 1964, p. 13.
They hold Christ up for ascension

C-193 AND HE FED THEM ALL
Spirit 31, May 1964, pp. 45-46.
Looking out upon that throng

C-194 I ENCOUNTER MEN IN THE WORLD
Spirit 31, May 1964, p. 46.
hopelessness stands in their eyes

C-195 THE SEASON OF YOUTH / (REVIEW OF *SMALL RAIN* BY RAYMOND
ROSELIEP)
Today 19, May 1964, pp. 29-30.

C-196 THE SISTINE CHAPEL
Spirit 31, May 1964, p. 47.
Illusory, a maelstrom of wrong purpose

C-197 THE SPIRIT OF YOUTH [III]
Queen's Work 56, May 1964, pp. 20-23.

C-198 YEAR OF OUR LORD (ALGERIA, 1961)
Spirit 31, May 1964, pp. 46-47.
Turmoil, day labor,

C-199 THE CONTEMPORARY CHRISTIAN / [EXPLORING OUR FREEDOM
III]
Today 19, June 1964, pp. 18-20.

Art by Petrie Joan Bertolis.

C-200 [LETTER TO DOROTHY DAY]
Catholic Worker, June 1964, p. 5.

Unsigned.

C-201   THE MISSION OF THE CHURCH
        YCS International Review, June 1964.

C-202   THE TEST
        Sponsa Regis 35, June 1964, p. 340.
        With serious intent He created

C-203   THE EIGHT HUNDRED YEARS OF NOTRE DAME
        Critic 22, June-July 1964, p. 30-38.

C-204   AIR MAIL LETTER
        Ave Maria 99, 27 June 1964, p. 8.
        A brutal landscape, they say,

C-205   A BEGGAR, FIRST
        Ave Maria 99, 27 June 1964, p. 5.
        Sometimes, misery has beauty to commend it.

C-206   IMMANENCE
        Ave Maria 99, 27 June 1964, p. 5.
        I see You in the world--

C-207   PARIS DIARY
        Ave Maria 99, 27 June 1964, pp. 5-8.

        Illustrations by Zygmund Jankowski. See individual
        entries for A BEGGAR, FIRST; IMMANENCE; A THRUSH IN
        THE CITY; SAINT SULPICE; A VIEW FROM A SIDE STREET;
        PARIS, YOU COULD PRESS WINE FROM THISTLES; UNFINISHED
        LINES; AIR MAIL LETTER.

C-208   PARIS, YOU COULD PRESS WINE FROM THISTLES
        Ave Maria 99, 27 June 1964, p. 7.
        make easter eggs of gutter stones

C-209   SAINT SULPICE
        Ave Maria 99, 27 June 1964, p. 6.
        In the botched barracks, coming on

C-210   A THRUSH IN THE CITY
        Ave Maria 99, 27 June 1964, p. 6.
        purity of heart

C-211   UNFINISHED LINES
        Ave Maria 99, 27 June 1964, p. 7.
        October brings leaves down

C-212 A VIEW FROM A SIDE STREET
       Ave Maria 99, 27 June 1964, p. 6.
       The streets shouldering awkwardly along

C-213 THE CHURCH IN THE MODERN WORLD
       Challenge, July 1964, pp. 3-7.

C-214 THE NEWSSTAND
       Ave Maria 100, 22 August 1964, p. 25.
       In cold November

       Illustrated by Zygmund Jankowski.

C-215 THE MISSION OF THE CHURCH
       Perspectives 9, September-October 1964, pp. 137-143.

C-216 A COMMUNITY ON MISSION
       Jesuit Missions 38, October 1964, pp. 14-15.

C-217 HOLY COMMUNION (FOR MIKE)
       Catholic Worker, October 1964, p. 5.
       He took his ration

C-218 TRAVELERS
       Catholic Worker, October 1964, p. 4.
       If geography's the tip of someone's

C-219 HOW STRANGE THE WORLD
       Commonweal 81, 30 October 1964, p. 155.
       Richness, strangeness, depth;

C-220 POOR, FREE EVER MAKING CHANGE--AN EMERGENT CHURCH
          TAKES FORM
       Unity, November 1964, pp. 1, 3, 4.

       Notes taken at a conference by Daniel Berrigan in
       Montreal after a European sabbatical. Writer is
       Mary MacAsey.

C-221 POVERTY
       Jesuit Missions 38, November 1964, pp. 1-2.

C-222 THE CHILDREN
       Jesuit Missions 38, December 1964, pp. 6-7.

C-223 WHAT DO WE HOPE FOR, FOR THE CHILDREN?
       Jesuit Missions 38, December 1964, p. 7.
       Once on a night, Saint Luke wrote

1965

C-224   FIDELITY TO THE LIVING: REFLECTIONS
        Continuum 3, Spring 1965, pp. 105-115.

C-225   KEEP THE HOUR
        Continuum 3, Spring 1965, p. 103.
        I set this down toward May midnight

C-226   POEM (from Jacopone da Todi)
        Continuum 3, Summer 1965, p. 221.
        In my morning prayer

C-227   THE PROPHETIC MINISTRY
        Continuum 3, Summer 1965, pp. 252-254.

        Co-authored with Philip Berrigan.

C-228   FIDELITY TO THE LIVING   II: REFLECTIONS
        Continuum 3, Autumn 1965, pp. 370-378.

C-229   DACHAU IS NOW OPEN FOR VISITORS
        Continuum 2, Winter 1965, p. 681.
        The arabesque scrawled by the dead

C-230   IN THE CHILDREN'S WARD
        Continuum 2, Winter 1965, p. 680.
        I was pondering no mystery

C-231   MIRACLES
        Woodstock Letters 94, Winter 1965, p. 23.
        Were I God almighty, I would ordain

C-232   TO A DEAD POET, HIS BOOK
        Woodstock Letters 94, Winter 1965, p. 22.
        It is a doorway to seasons; it makes

C-233   LORD AND SERVANT OF HISTORY
        Jesuit Missions 39, January-February 1965, p. 28.

C-234   THE OTHER WORLD AND POOR AMERICA
        *A[ssociation] [for] I[nternational] D[evelopment] Dia-
        logue* 2, January-February 1965, pp. 1-6.

C-235   THE 20th CENTURY POOR: MORE AND WORSE--
        Unity, February 1965, pp. 1-4.

C-236 IN PEACEABLE CONFLICT
Catholic Worker, March 1965, pp. 1, 7.

C-237 LENT IS THE WORLD: LIFE, DEATH AND NEW LIFE ONCE MORE
Jesuit Missions 39, March 1965, p. 13.
It is the drama

C-238 BORN IN A GRAVE
Jesuit Missions 39, April 1965, pp. 2-3.

C-239 THE POOR MAN IS IN FACT ALL MEN
Unity, April 1965, pp. 1-4.

C-240 WHO IS DEPRIVED?
Commonweal 82, 2 April 1965, pp. 53-55.

C-241 SELMA AND SHARPEVILLE
Commonweal 82, 9 April 1965, pp. 71-75.

C-242 TO THE STATE PRESIDENT, CAPETOWN, SOUTH AFRICA
Ave Maria 101, 10 April 1965, pp. 16-17.

C-243 MAN'S SPIRIT AND TECHNOLOGY
Fellowship 31, May 1965, pp. 22-26.

C-244 SELMA REMEMBERED
Jesuit Missions 39, May 1965, p. 3.

C-245 SERVANT OF THE SLAVE
Jesuit Missions 39, May 1965, pp. 6-9.

C-246 TOTAL WAR IS A TOTAL GOD
Unity, May 1965, pp. 1-4.

C-247 THE OTHER WORLD AND POOR AMERICA
Ave Maria 101, 22 May 1965, pp. 5-8.

C-248 THE INDIFFERENT SOCIETY OR A DIFFERENT ONE
Jesuit Missions 39, June 1965, pp. 24-25.

C-249 CHRISTIAN HEROISM
Catholic Messenger, [ca. 25 June 1965].
Wrong date--unable to trace.

C-250 RUSSIAN JOURNEY
Critic 23, June-July 1965, pp. 52-56.

C-251   A CHILD WRITES
        Jesuit Missions 39, July–August 1965, p. 2.
        When a child writes

        Unsigned, DB a possible author.

C-252   THE YOUNG MAN AND THE SEA
        Jesuit Missions 39, July–August 1965, pp. 11–12.
        When God shows His power

C-253   FROM FENCE AND FREEHOLD TO THE SEA
        Jesuit Missions 39, September 1965, pp. 6–9.

C-254   FATHER DANIEL BERRIGAN: INTERVIEW WITH A DISSENTER ON
            VIETNAM
        National Catholic Reporter, 8 September 1965, p. 2.

C-255   QUESTION
        Christian Century 82, 22 September 1965, p. 1187.
        If the world's temperate zone,

C-256   CLUNY MUSEUM
        Motive 26, October 1965, p. 47.
        The woman's hands weave

C-257   A MAN BORN BLIND
        Jesuit Missions 39, October 1965, pp. 22–23.

        Illustrated by Sister Photina.

C-258   A POOR MAN'S SLEEP (GOD SAYS)
        Jesuit Missions 39, October 1965, p. [38].
        A poor man's sleep (God says)

        Unsigned, DB a possible author.

C-259   ALL SAINTS AND ALL MEN
        Jesuit Missions 39, November 1965, pp. 16–21.

C-260   THE OTHER AMERICA AND THE OTHER WORLD
        Catholic Mind 63, November 1965, pp. 20–28.

C-261   TECHNOLOGY AND THE SPIRIT OF MAN
        Worldview 8, November 1965, pp. 5–8.

C-262   I COME AS A MESSENGER AND BROTHER
        Jesuit Missions 39, December 1965, pp. 10–15.

C-263   SERMON FOR A MODERN MARTYR
        Unity, December 1965, pp. 1, 3, 4.

C-264 [WHEN I HEAR BREAD BREAKING....]
Jesuit Missions 39, December 1965, pp. 18-19.

Seriograph by Corita [Kent].

C-265 ....IN A SICK HUMAN BEING
National Catholic Reporter, 22 December 1965, p. 5.

C-266 FATHER BERRIGAN SPEAKS FOR HIMSELF
Commonweal 83, 24 December 1965, p. 362.

1966

C-267 FIDELITY TO THE LIVING III: REFLECTIONS
Continuum 4, Spring 1966, pp. 116-125.

C-268 ACT OF FAITH AND THE NEW BEAST
Fellowship 32, January 1966, pp. 19-24.

Sequel to MAN'S SPIRIT AND TECHNOLOGY.

C-269 REFLECTIONS ON THE PRIEST AS PEACEMAKER
Jubilee 13, February 1966, pp. 22-29.

C-270 POEMS
Critic 24, February-March 1966, pp. 40-48.

Illustrated by [Sr.] Mary Corita [Kent]. See individ-
ual entries for SUBURBAN PRAYER, PRAYER ON THE SIX
P.M. SUBWAY, PRAYER OF THE THIRD MAN, PRAYER FROM THE
CATBIRD SEAT, PRAYER FROM A PICKET LINE, PRAYER FROM
A BACK PEW, PRAYER FOR THE MORNING HEADLINES, PRAYER
FOR THE BIG MORNING.

C-271 PRAYER FOR THE BIG MORNING
Critic 24, February-March 1966, p. 48.
People my heart

C-272 PRAYER FOR THE MORNING HEADLINES
Critic 24, February-March, 1966, p. 48.
Mercifully grant peace in our days. Through your
  help may we be freed from pres- [sic]

C-273 PRAYER FROM A BACK PEW
Critic 24, February-March 1966, p. 47.
Well I don't know, at least I wonder. One kid dead,
  the old

C-274   PRAYER FROM A PICKET LINE
        Critic 24, February–March 1966, p. 46.
        Bring the big guardian

C-275   PRAYER FROM THE CATBIRD SEAT
        Critic 24, February–March 1966, pp. 44–45.
        My God

C-276   PRAYER OF THE THIRD MAN
        Critic 24, February–March 1966, p. 43.
        I passed the wounded phoenix in the ditch, passed him
          twice; two aeons, two sins. A third time, it

C-277   PRAYER ON THE SIX P.M. SUBWAY
        Critic 24, February–March 1966, p. 42.
        Unsteady

C-278   SUBURBAN PRAYER
        Critic 24, February–March 1966, p. 41.
        Grant us for grace

C-279   [FATHER DAN WRITES FROM BRAZIL] / [LETTER TO TONY WALSH
          FROM BRAZIL]
        Unity, March 1966, pp. 1–4.

C-280   HELDER CAMARA: VOICE OF THE FUTURE
        Jesuit Missions 40, March 1966, pp. 2–9.

        Unsigned, DB a possible author.

C-281   THE HOUSE OF CARDS
        Jesuit Missions 40, March 1966, pp. 12–15.

C-282   [UNTIL]
        Jesuit Missions 40, March 1966, p. [28].
        The distance is not great---

C-283   DAY OF DAYS
        Jesuit Missions 40, April 1966, pp. 2–11.

C-284   JOURNEY INTO HOPE
        Jesuit Missions 40, May 1966, pp. 10–18 (insert).

C-285   JUNE
        Jesuit Missions 40, June 1966, p. 1.

C-286   TO LIMBO AND BACK: A LATIN AMERICAN JOURNEY
        Jubilee 14, July 1966, pp. 12–19.

C-287 A HAND OUTSTRETCHED
       Jesuit Missions 40, July-August 1966, pp. 12-19.

C-288 THE CHURCH AT THE EDGE
       Jesuit Missions 40, September 1966, pp. 12-19.

       Co-authored with Alden J. Stevenson, S.J.

C-289 FATHER DANIEL J. BERRIGAN, S.J.: ON FREEDOM, VIETNAM,
          SPIRITUALITY, RETREATS, AND THE CHURCH IN OKLAHOMA
       Oklahoma Courier, 13 November 1966, pp. 13-15.

       Interview with Mike McCarville.

C-290 THE G.I. WHO WOULDN'T CRY "KILL"
       National Catholic Reporter, 23 November 1966, p. 6.

C-291 WHERE IN THE WORLD IS HE?
       Jesuit Missions 40, December 1966, pp. 2-9.

C-292 MEDITATIONS ON A PHOTOGRAPH
       National Catholic Reporter, 21 December 1966, p. 1.

                              1967

C-293 FIDELITY TO THE LIVING IV: REFLECTIONS
       Continuum 5, Winter 1966-Spring 1967, pp. 153-159.

C-294 INTERNATIONAL LIFE AND PEACE: WHICH WAY TO REALITY?
       Katallagete [1], Winter 1966-1967, pp. 32-37.

C-295 FOOTNOTES, FANCY FREE
       Continuum 5, Summer 1967, pp. 365-370.
       The worst thing is an omnivorous solemnity

C-296 AND WHAT IS MAN
       Continuum 5, Autumn 1967, p. 574.
       Not like the rich

C-297 THE MESSAGE IS THE MEDIUM
       Continuum 5, Autumn 1967, p. 575.
       I feel sometimes

C-298 COME ALIVE
       Thought 42, Winter 1967, p. 617.
       I had lost everything for a year

C-299   FACING IT
        Thought 42, Winter 1967, p. 616.
        Who could declare your death, standing

C-300   FOUR POEMS
        Thought 42, Winter 1967, pp. 615–617.

        See individual entries for PEACEMAKING IS HARD, FACING
        IT, COME ALIVE, JOHN ANDERSON MY JO JOHN.

C-301   JOHN ANDERSON MY JO JOHN
        Thought 42, Winter 1967, p. 617.
        Men cannot pluck or wear

C-302   PEACEMAKING IS HARD
        Thought 42, Winter 1967, p. 615.
        hard almost as war

C-303   AFRICA: A PEOPLE'S ART
        Jesuit Missions 41, January–February 1967, pp. 22–27.

        Co-authored with H.B. Furay, S.J.

C-304   ALAS!
        Critic 25, April–May 1967, p. 26.

C-305   THE BOY AND THE TIGER
        Critic 25, April–May 1967, p. 23.

C-306   DEATH AND THE BISHOP
        Critic 25, April–May 1967, p. 22.

C-307   THE FIRST DAYS OF THE SCIENCE OF PRENATAL COMMUNICATION
        Critic 25, April–May 1967, pp. 28–29.

C-308   IRENE
        Critic 25, April–May 1967, p. 21.

C-309   SEVEN FABLES FOR OUR TIME
        Critic 25, April–May 1967, pp. 20–29.

        Drawings by Marilyn Fitscheu; photo by Thomas Brennan.
        See individual entries for IRENE, DEATH AND THE BISHOP,
        THE BOY AND THE TIGER, THE STATUE, ALAS!, THE SHOES
        THAT FAILED, THE FIRST DAYS OF THE SCIENCE OF PRENATAL
        COMMUNICATION.

C-310   THE SHOES THAT FAILED
        Critic 25, April–May 1967, p. 27.

C-311 THE STATUE
      Critic 25, April–May 1967, p. 25.

C-312 PAUPERES SEMPER: A NON–ENCYCLICAL
      Jesuit Missions 41, June 1967, pp. 13–18.

C-313 REFLECTIONS ON A TROUBLED WORLD
      Christian Advocate 11, 1 June 1967, pp. 11–12.

C-314 THE TENSION BETWEEN ART AND FAITH
      Critic 26, August–September 1967, pp. 32–37.

C-315 ICTHUS
      Catholic Peace Fellowship Bulletin, September 1967,
        pp. 5–7.

C-316 A NON–SERMON
      Fellowship 33, September 1967, pp. 13–14.

C-317 SOMEWHERE THE EQUATION BREAKS DOWN
      New Yorker 43, 9 September 1967, p. 49.
      between the perfect

C-318 THIS CRUCIFIX
      Poetry 111, October 1967, p. 33.
      never eased life with miracles

C-319 I AM NEVER COMPLETE
      Poetry 111, October 1967, p. 31.
      A man, a woman, their love

C-320 OF FAIR LOVE THE MOTHER
      Poetry 111, October 1967, p. 32.
      Panic of dark minds sounds

C-321 SOMEHOW
      Poetry 111, October 1967, p. 33.
      I kiss a book sometimes

C-322 THE UNFINISHED MAN
      Poetry 111, October 1967, p. 32.
      walks with his winter shadow.

C-323 THE WEDDING
      Poetry 111, October 1967, pp. 34–35.
      Make way, make way! the poor

C-324   EDIFICES
        Motive 28, November 1967, p. 47.

        See separate listings for ON THE TURNPIKE and THE WALL.

C-325   ON THE TURNPIKE
        Motive 28, November 1967, p. 47.
        Who loaded history's pig iron

C-326   SORROW
        Unity, November 1967, p. 2.
        I saw a mother mourning her sick child

C-327   THE WALL
        Motive 28, November 1967, p. 47.
        It was in no sense shoring up the wall

C-328   "END THE WAR" MESSAGE IS SENT TO VIETS BY BERRIGANS
        Catholic Messenger, 30 November 1967, p. 12.

        Co-authored with Philip Berrigan.

C-329   LETTER FROM THREE JAILS
        National Catholic Reporter, 20 December 1967, p. 6.

                                1968

C-330   CONVERSATIONS ON NORTH VIETNAM
        First Issue, [Ithaca, N.Y., ca. 1968], pp. 11-14.

        With Pat Griffith.

C-331   THE BEST OF TIMES: THE WORST OF TIMES
        Continuum 6, Summer 1968, pp. 249-253.

C-332   THE "WHY" BEHIND CIVIL DISOBEDIENCE AT CATONSVILLE
        Cornell Law Forum 21, Fall 1968, pp. 5, 18-19.

        With Robert Semmer.

C-333   OPEN SESAME: MY LIFE AND GOOD TIMES
        Katallagete 2, Winter 1968-1969, pp. 19-25.

C-334   LETTER FROM THREE JAILS
        Unity, January-February 1968, p. 1.

C-335   BERRIGAN AT CORNELL
        Jubilee 15, February 1968, pp. 28-36.

        With photographs.

C-336   ALERT
        Liberation 22, March 1968, p. 29.
        The sirens are loosed on Hanoi

C-337   BOMBARDMENT
        Liberation 22, March 1968, p. 31.
        Like those who go aground

C-338   CHILDREN IN THE SHELTER
        Liberation 22, March 1968, p. 31.
        Imagine; three of them

C-339   CUERNAVACA REVISITED
        Jubilee 15, March 1968, pp. 34-40.

C-340   DARKNESS, THE NIGHT FLIGHT TO HANOI
        Liberation 22, March 1968, p. 28.
        In a bar in Vientiane

C-341   FLOWERS
        Liberation 22, March 1968, p. 32.
        A flower is single jeopardy

C-342   JOURNEY TO HANOI: A POETRY READING
        Liberation 22, March 1968, pp. 26-35.

        See individual entries for ALERT; BOMBARDMENT; CHIL-
        DREN IN THE SHELTER; DARKNESS, THE NIGHT FLIGHT TO
        HANOI; FLOWERS; PRAYER; PROGRESS IN RURAL DEVELOPMENT:
        A LECTURE ON PRIVIES, AND A GIFT TO OUR COUNTRYMEN;
        SONG; WAITING: (VIENTIANE) (with comments on his trip
        to Hanoi).

C-343   PRAYER
        Liberation 22, March 1968, p. 28.
        I left Cornell

C-344   PROGRESS IN RURAL DEVELOPMENT: A LECTURE ON PRIVIES,
          AND A GIFT TO OUR COUNTRYMEN
        Liberation 22, March 1968, p. 35.
        In the municipal hospital, in the bone-chilling cold

C-345 SONG
       Liberation 22, March 1968, p. 32.
       The maids sing at their scrubbing

C-346 WAITING: (VIENTIANE)
       Liberation 22, March 1968, p. 27.
       The birds of dawn are crying, drawing

C-347 FATHER DANIEL BERRIGAN ON HIS TRIP TO HANOI
       America 118, 9 March 1968, pp. 320-324.

C-348 FATHER DAN BERRIGAN--BACK FROM HANOI
       National Catholic Reporter, 13 March 1968, p. 2.

C-349 MISSION TO HANOI [I]
       Worldview 11, April 1968, pp. 6-11.

C-350 DEAR SISTERS: DON'T SLIP, DON'T FOLD, KEEP SMILING
       National Catholic Reporter, 3 April 1968, p. 4.

C-351 THE FOURTH R: RESISTANCE
       NASPA [The Journal of the Association of Deans and
          Administrators of Student Affairs], 4 April 1968,
          pp. 316-320.

C-352 MY BROTHER, THE WITNESS
       Commonweal 88, 26 April 1968, pp. 180-182.

C-353 MISSION TO HANOI   II
       Worldview 11, May 1968, pp. 11-15.

C-354 DANIEL BERRIGAN: A MEDITATION
       National Catholic Reporter, 29 May 1968, p. 6.

C-355 WHY WE BURN DRAFT RECORDS
       National Catholic Reporter, 29 May 1968, p. 6.

C-356 DANIEL BERRIGAN ANSWERS ROSEMARY RUETHER
       National Catholic Reporter, 19 June 1968, p. 4.

C-357 SAY NO!
       Catholic Radical, September 1968, pp. 3-4.

C-358 AN INVITATION FROM CATONSVILLE NINE
       National Catholic Reporter, 25 September 1968, p. 4.

       Co-authored with the Catonsville Nine.

C-359 FROM THE CATONSVILLE NINE: GREETINGS
      Commonweal 88, 27 September 1968, p. 646.

      Co-authored with the Catonsville 9.

C-360 A MEDITATION
      Unity, October 1968, p. 2.

C-361 LETTER TO BE SENT EVERYWHERE
      Ave Maria 108, 5 October 1968, p. 31.

      Includes PEACEMAKING IS HARD.

C-362 BERRIGAN ON (IN/OUT OF) BALTIMORE
      Dateline: Ithaca, [Ithaca, N.Y.] 23 October 1968,
        pp. 4, 6.

      With Daniel Finlay.

C-363 TRIAL POEM #6 / CATONSVILLE NINE: STATEMENTS AT
        SENTENCING
      National Catholic Reporter, 20 November 1968, p. 4.
      IN OUR BIG CRUEL WARD

      Includes statements by members of the Catonsville 9,
      pp. 4-5.

1969

C-364 AT THE TIME OF HIS DEATH, AMERICANS HAD MASTERED THE
        DYNAMICS OF A MOON FLIGHT
      Continuum 7, Summer 1969, p. 315.
      Merton's gone; that comfort ended

C-365 EDIFYING ANECDOTES CONCERNING THE DECEASED ARE NOW IN
        ORDER
      Continuum 7, Summer 1969, p. 316.
      A sick woman

C-366 MEMORIES AFTER THE FACT: A VISIT OF ILL-FAVORED
        CHARACTERS TO THE MONASTERY
      Continuum 7, Summer 1969, p. 317.
      Under the stars, a last beer

C-367 1969 OPENED LIKE THIS
      Continuum 7, Summer 1969, p. 314.
      I wish I had some joy----

C-368   "THE TRAPPIST CEMETERY--GETHSEMANI" REVISITED
        Continuum 7, Summer 1969, pp. 313-318.

        See individual entries for 1969 OPENED LIKE THIS; AT
        THE TIME OF HIS DEATH, AMERICANS HAD MASTERED THE DY-
        NAMICS OF A MOON FLIGHT; EDIFYING ANECDOTES CONCERNING
        THE DECEASED ARE NOW IN ORDER; MEMORIES AFTER THE
        FACT: A VISIT OF ILL-FAVORED CHARACTERS TO THE MONAS-
        TERY; WHO'S WHO AT THE OBSEQUIES.

C-369   WHO'S WHO AT THE OBSEQUIES
        Continuum 7, Summer 1969, p. 318.
        General Hershey did not mourn

C-370   VALUES AND THE UNIVERSITY
        Katallagete 2, Fall 1969, pp. 27-29.

C-371   THE WOMAN WHO WAS POOR
        Unity, January 1969, p. 2.

C-372   EXIT THE KING AND THE CRISIS OF AMERICA
        Ark [Cornell United Religious Work] 1, February 1969,
           pp. 15-19.

C-373   THE FUNERAL ORATION OF THOMAS MERTON AS PRONOUNCED BY
           THE COMPASSIONATE BUDDHA
        Catholic Worker, February 1969, p. 5.
        Assembled sirs. The courtesies afforded us by the
           Dalai Lama,

C-374   TRIAL BY FIRE
        Motive 29, February 1969, pp. 34-38.

        Illustrations by Tom Lewis.

C-375   EXIT THE KING AND CRISIS OF AMERICA
        Critic 27, February-March 1969, pp. 20-25.

C-376   LAST DAY
        Unity, March 1969, p. 4.
        When He did come, all the

C-377   THIS MAN IS ARMED: THE CLEAVER OF ELDRIDGE [Review of
        Soul on Ice by Eldridge Cleaver]
        National Catholic Reporter, 19 March 1969, p. 11.

C-378   A EULOGY TO THOMAS MERTON AS DELIVERED BY THE COM-
           PASSIONATE BUDDHA
        Rising Sun [Temple University], May 1969, pp. 12-13.

Assembled sirs. The courtesies afforded us by the
    Dalai Lama,

C-379 A RAP ON RELIGION
       Fortnight [Cornell University], 14 May 1969, pp. 6-8,
         12.

C-380 CONSCIENCE, LAW AND CIVIL DISOBEDIENCE
       U.S. Catholic 34, July 1969, pp. 19-22.

C-381 COLLEGIANS--FATHER DANIEL BERRIGAN
       National Catholic Reporter, 16 July 1969, p. 7.

C-382 THE FUTURE: A VISION
       Catholic Radical, August 1969, p. 3.

C-383 PRAYER OF DAN BERRIGAN
       Catonsville Roadrunner, September 1969, unpaginated.

C-384 THE IMPULSE THAT BRINGS *YEAR ONE* INTO EXISTENCE
       Year One [Ithaca, N.Y.], October 1969.

C-385 A MEDITATION ON A GREEDY PEOPLE
       National Catholic Reporter, 8 October 1969, p. 8.

C-386 AN INTERVIEW WITH DAN BERRIGAN
       East Hill Newspaper [East Hill School, Ithaca, N.Y.],
         9 October 1969, p. 3.

       With Melanie Smith.

C-387 THE BISHOP AND THE GHOSTS OF FILETTO
       Commonweal 91, 10 October 1969, pp. 39-42.

       Includes poem, [YOUR EXCELLENCY]; see individual
       entry.

C-388 [YOUR EXCELLENCY]
       Commonweal 91, 10 October 1969, pp. 39-40.
       Your Excellency

C-389 HOW DOES IT FEEL TO BE FACING JAIL?
       Lamp 67, November 1969, pp. 2-5.
       People ask me continually

C-390 DAVE DARST MEMORIAL
       Catholic Radical, December 1969, pp. 6-7.

C-391   THE LONG DEFEAT OF SOMETHING WELL DONE
        Year One [Ithaca, N.Y.], 3, December 1969–January
            1970, pp. 4–30.

                              1970

C-392   FOR DAVID DARST FSC
        Continuum 8, Spring–Summer 1970, pp. 141–150.

C-393   PRAYER OF DAN BERRIGAN
        Episcopal Peace Fellowship Newsletter, Summer 1970,
            p. 20.
        We pray the God of peace

C-394   THE PATH OF GREATEST RESISTANCE
        U.S. Catholic 35, January 1970, pp. 6–11.

        With Harry Cargas.

C-395   A REPORT ON DANIEL LANG'S "CASUALTIES OF WAR"
        Catholic Radical, February 1970, pp. 4–5.

C-396   ULYSSES OF ITHACA, NEW YORK SUTRA FOR THE NEW TERM
        Cornell Daily Sun, 4 February 1970, p. 7.
        carried typhoid germs

        Illustrations by Steve Burklund.

C-397   THE NEW MAN: THE COMPLEAT SOLDIER
        Saturday Review 53, 14 February 1970, pp. 31–34, 42–43.

C-398   I AM PRIVILEGED TO VISIT ONCE MORE THE GOLDEN DOME AND
            FIND IT STILL AT HOME FOR WHICH THANK YOU FATHER
            HESBURGH
        Scholastic [Notre Dame University] 31, 20 February
            1970, p. 21.
        The Golden Dome, the forehead of God the Father by

C-399   FOR THE WEDDING DECEMBER 20, 1969
        Liberation 15, March 1970, pp. 16–17.
        Tom and Stasia are marrying

C-400   [I HAVE A MAN]
        Cornell Daily Sun, 25 March 1970, p. 9.
        I have a man

C-401 MAYBE THE LAST TIME....
Cornell Daily Sun, 27 March 1970, p. 4.
Coming in by Slowhawk airlines   Thursday last

C-402 ON ELBOW ROOM BREATHING SPACE AND BEING LET ALONE;
GRAFFITI FOR THE BROKEN FENCES AND BREACHED WALLS OF
A LIBERATED PEOPLES' PARK IN FEALTY TO *JESUS* WHOSE
IDEA IT WAS IN THE FIRST PLACE AND WHO GOT THE PEO-
PLE MOVING
Critic 28, March-April 1970, pp. 31-39.

Copied out by Corita Kent.

C-403 REVOLUTION
Critic 28, March-April 1970, p. 34.
the egg stands on its head

C-404 AMERICA IS HARD TO FIND
Cornell Daily Sun, 17 April 1970 [p. 3] [special
section].
Hard to find;

C-405 LETTER TO THE JESUITS
National Catholic Reporter, 24 April 1970, p. 5.

C-406 LOOKING AT CATONSVILLE
Worldview 13, May 1970, pp. 6-9.

C-407 NOTES FROM THE UNDERGROUND; OR, I WAS A FUGITIVE FROM
THE F.B.I.
Commonweal 92, 29 May 1970, pp. 263-265.

C-408 PASSION OF DIETRICH BONHOEFFER
Saturday Review 53, 30 May 1970, pp. 17-22.
I begin these notes on 9 April 1970.   Two hours ago,
at 8:30 A.M.,

C-409 FROM THE UNDERGROUND   I
Fellowship Peace Information Edition, June 1970, p. 7.

C-410 TWICE-BORN MEN: THE UNMASKING OF FEAR
Village Voice, 4 June 1970, pp. 5-6, 39.

C-411 LIFE AT THE EDGE
Christian Century 87, 24 June 1970, pp. 787-790.

C-412 NOW YOU SEE HIM
Harry, 17 July 1970, p. 3.

C-413   NOTES FROM THE UNDERGROUND
        New Yorker 46, 25 July 1970, pp. 20-23.

C-414   HOW TO MAKE A DIFFERENCE
        Commonweal 92, 7 August 1970, pp. 384-386.

C-415   LETTERS FROM THE UNDERGROUND
        New York Review of Books, 13 August 1970, pp. 34-35.

C-416   TEMPTATIONS A REVOLUTIONARY ENCOUNTERS
        Time, 24 August 1970, p. 48.

C-417   IT IS VERY NECESSARY TO SPEAK PLAINLY
        Harry, 18 September 1970, p. 14.

C-418   FATHER DAN BERRIGAN: THE HOLY OUTLAW
        Christianity and Crisis 30, 21 September 1970, pp.
          184-185.

        Includes poems THINGS HOPED FOR and CHILDREN IN A
        SHELTER.

C-419   HOW TO MAKE A DIFFERENCE
        Current 122, October 1970, pp. 25-27.

C-420   NOTES FROM THE UNDERGROUND
        New Blackfriars 51, October 1970, pp. 454-461.

C-421   ON "THE DARK NIGHT OF THE SOUL"
        New York Review of Books, 22 October 1970, pp. 10-11.

C-422   LET US BE MEN: THE LAST UNDERGROUND SPEECH
        Motive 31, November 1970, pp. 20-21.

C-423   SERMON BY DANIEL BERRIGAN AUGUST 2, 1970
        Motive 31, November 1970, pp. 27-32.

C-424   TEXT OF BERRIGANS' PRISON SERMON
        National Catholic Reporter, 20 November 1970, p. 12.

        With Philip Berrigan.

C-425   [LETTER TO JUDGE ROSZEL THOMSEN]
        New York *Times*, 14 December 1970, p. 43.

1971

C-426 FATHER BERRIGAN'S LETTER TO THE WEATHERMEN
       Village Voice, 21 January 1971, p. 7.

C-427 A SERMON FROM JAIL
       Chinook, 21 January 1971, p. 1.

C-428 FROM UNDERGROUND, FATHER BERRIGAN SPEAKS TO ACTORS
       New York *Times*, 31 January 1971, p. 13.

C-429 LETTER TO THE WEATHERMEN
       Catholic Agitator, February 1971, pp. 1, 7+.

C-430 PRAYER FROM THE CATBIRD SEAT
       Inside Magazine 69, 2 February 1971, p. 5.
       will you for a space of days

C-431 "DEAR BROTHERS AND SISTERS, THIS IS DAN BERRIGAN
          SPEAKING, I WANT TO SAY"
       Community Action Newsletter 3, March 1971, pp. 1-4.

C-432 A DIALOGUE UNDERGROUND: I
       New York Review of Books, 11 March 1971, pp. 19-27.

       1st of 3; with Robert Coles.

C-433 DIALOGUE WITH RADICAL PRIEST DANIEL BERRIGAN.
       Time, 22 March 1971, pp. 16-17.

       With Robert Coles.

C-434 A DIALOGUE UNDERGROUND: II
       New York Review of Books, 25 March 1971, pp. 24-30.

       2nd of 3; with Robert Coles.

C-435 A DIALOGUE UNDERGROUND: III
       New York Review of Books, 8 April 1971, pp. 12-21.
       Inside and Outside the Church

       3rd of 3; with Robert Coles.

C-436 DARKNESS, DARKNESS, DARKNESS, HOW ABOUT SOME LIGHT
       Critic 29, May-June 1971, pp. 44-49.

       Graphics by Corita Kent.

C-437   A LETTER FROM JAIL
        National Catholic Reporter, 24 September 1971, p. 16.

C-438   TO: J. EDGAR HOOVER / FROM: DANIEL BERRIGAN
        Harrisburg *Independent Press* 1, November 1971, pp. 3,
            5, 18-24.

C-439   LOVE LETTER TO J. EDGAR HOOVER
        National Catholic Reporter, 26 November 1971, p. 14.

C-440   OF COURSE WE ARE UGLY BUT AGAIN IT MAY BE YOUR
        Folio [Pacifica (KPFK) Foundation], December 1971,
            p. 4.
        of course we are ugly but again it may be your

C-441   A LETTER FROM THE BERRIGANS
        American Report, 31 December 1971, p. 5.

        With Philip Berrigan.

                                1972

C-442   [2] [MIGHT BE ONE OF THOSE MIGHTY GODS IN THE OLD ZEN
            TALES]
        Unmuzzled Ox 1, Autumn 1972, unpaginated.
        Might be one of those mighty gods in the old Zen tales

C-443   [6] [NOW WHAT THE HELL SORT OF]
        Unmuzzled Ox 1, Autumn 1972, unpaginated.
        Now what the hell sort of

C-444   [4] [QUERY: SHALL A MAN THEN RETURN]
        Unmuzzled Ox 1, Autumn 1972, unpaginated.
        QUERY: Shall a man then return

C-445   SOME POEMS FROM UNDERGROUND: 1970
        Unmuzzled Ox 1, Autumn 1972, unpaginated.

        See individual entries for THAT DIVINE IDEA; MIGHT BE
        ONE OF THOSE MIGHTY GODS IN THE OLD ZEN TALES; WARNING:
        MUST LEARN TO GO; QUERY: SHALL A MAN THEN RETURN;
        THURSDAY A WEEK OR WEATHER FORBIDDING, SUNDAY; NOW
        WHAT THE HELL SORT OF.

C-446   [1] [THAT DIVINE IDEA]
        Unmuzzled Ox 1, Autumn 1972, unpaginated.
        That divine idea

C-447   [8] [THURSDAY A WEEK OR WEATHER FORBIDDING, SUNDAY]
        Unmuzzled Ox 1, Autumn 1972, unpaginated.
        Thursday a week or weather forbidding, Sunday

C-448   [3] [WARNING: MUST LEARN TO GO]
        Unmuzzled Ox 1, Autumn 1972, unpaginated.
        WARNING: must learn to go

C-449   PEACE, PEACE--BUT THERE IS NO PEACE
        U.S. Catholic and Jubilee 37, June 1972, pp. 25-32.

        Illustrations by Corita Kent.

C-450   STREET WITHOUT JOY
        Movin' Together, July 1972, pp. 4-5.

C-451   IT'S NOT ENOUGH TO BE SYMPATHETIC
        Commonweal 96, 14 July 1972, pp. 376-382.

C-452   BROTHERHOOD OF PRISONERS; LETTERS FROM DANBURY, U.S.A.
           TO SIBERIA, U.S.S.R.
        Commonweal 96, September 1972, pp. 476-478.

C-453   A CALL TO ACTION
        Harrisburg *Independent Press*, October 1972, p. 4.

C-454   SLAVE CAMPS AND TIGER CAGES / LETTER TO LEONID BREZHNEV
        Village Voice, 5 October 1972, pp. 74-77.

C-455   DAN BERRIGAN SAYS: FIGHT BACK
        Omega Press 1, 20 December 1972, pp. 14-15.

                                1973

C-456   INTERVIEW
        Catonsville Roadrunner, issue 42 [ca. January 1973],
           unpaginated.

C-457   BERRIGAN AND THE BEAST:
        Peace News, 26 January 1973, p. 4.

C-458   DANIEL BERRIGAN ON THOMAS MERTON
        Thomas Merton Life Center Newsletter, April 1973,
           pp. 6, 7, 11.

C-459   BERRIGAN: ANOTHER STORY
        Manitoban, 12 April 1973, p. 3.

C-460   CONTEMPLATION AND RESISTANCE
        Peace News, 18 May 1973, pp. 5-8.

        With James Forest and Thich Nhat Hanh.

C-461   CONTEMPLATION AND RESISTANCE
        WIN 9, 14 June 1973, pp. 4-10.

        With Thich Nhat Hanh.

C-462   COMMENCEMENT, 1973
        New Yorker 49, 23 June 1973, pp. 28-30.

C-463   AN OPEN LETTER TO POLITICAL PRISONERS IN THE U.S.S.R.
        WIN 9, 28 June 1973, p. 9.

C-464   [MORE LIGHT, PLEASE]
        Harrisburg *Independent Press*, August 1973, p. 8.
        More light, please

C-465   "WE TOLD THEM ABOUT YOU, YURIY SHUKHEVYCH..."
        Fellowship 39, September 1973, pp. 4-5.

C-466   ON THE TORTURE OF PRISONERS
        Fellowship 39, September 1973, pp. 4-5.

C-467   RESPONSES TO SETTLER REGIMES
        American Report, 29 October 1973.

C-468   A LETTER TO VIETNAMESE PRISONERS
        Fellowship 39, November 1973, pp. 5-6.
        Dear Friends, your faces are a constriction of grief
           in the throat

C-469   THE HEROIC IDOL AND THE SLOUCHING BEAST
        Peace News, 16 November 1973, p. 5.

C-470   NOTES FROM THE UNDERGROUND
        Commonweal 99, 16 November 1973, pp. 186-187.

C-471   [LETTER TO *UNITY*]
        Unity, December 1973, p. 11.

C-472   PRISON: A PLACE WHERE DEATH DIDN'T QUITE MAKE IT
        Catholic Worker, December 1973, p. 4.
        So much death, death in official skulls

C-473 YEAR ONE
      Unity, December 1973, pp. 6-7.

1974

C-474 ON CELEBRATING OUR DEFEATS
      New Politics 11, Winter 1974, pp. 26-30.

C-475 [LETTER TO ROY PFAFF]
      American Report 4, 21 January 1974, pp. 10, 13.

C-476 THE MIDDLE EAST: SANE *SOLUTION*?
      Liberation 18, February 1974, pp. 8-13.

C-477 NOTES FROM PRISON
      Ramparts 12, February 1974, pp. 51-56.

C-478 AN AMERICAN VOICE ON SOVIET DISSIDENTS
      I.D.O.C. [*International Documentation of the Con-
        temporary Church*] *Bulletin*, number 17, March 1974,
      pp. 14-15.

C-479 DANIEL BERRIGAN AND HANS MORGENTHAU DISCUSS THE MORAL
        DILEMMA IN THE MIDDLE EAST...
      Progressive 38, 4 March 1974, pp. 31-34.

      Edited by J.H. Hamilton.

C-480 ALL HONOR TO THE WRONG PEOPLE
      WIN 10, 28 March 1974, pp. 14-15.

C-481 WITNESSES IN THE ENDLESS WINTER
      Catholic Worker, June 1974, pp. 1, 8.

C-482 "IN WAR, TRUTH IS THE FIRST CASUALTY"
      Fellowship 40, 12 June 1974.

      With Paul Mayer.

C-483 OPEN LETTER TO JOE O'ROURKE
      Commonweal 101, 18 October 1974.

C-484 REVOLUTION / RETALIATION [:] OR, HOW WE FINALLY DIS-
        POSED OF THE CHILDREN
      WIN 10, 30 October 1974, pp. 14-16, 18.

1975

C-485   A FRIEND WHO COULD NOT SLEEP
        Unmuzzled Ox 3 (2), 1975, pp. 70-73.
        You are condemned to the sleeplessness of god.

C-486   AMBITION
        Webster Review 2, Fall 1975, p. 17.
        I wanted to be useless

C-487   FIDELITY
        Webster Review 2, Fall 1975, pp. 12-14.
        Coming up Broadway, a fruitless evening

C-488   RICH WOMAN AT THE TICKET COUNTER
        Webster Review 2, Fall 1975, pp. 15-16.
        I see you

C-489   *A TIME TO DIE*, BY TOM WICKER. [review]
        Critic 34, Fall 1975, pp. 71-75.

C-490   NAMELESS ODE
        WIN 11, 20 March 1975, pp. 12-13.
        Like the blind man who sang Odysseus past the rocks
            and home free

C-491   FOR THE VIETNAMESE CHILDREN WHO PERISHED ON A FLIGHT
            FROM SAIGON APRIL 1975--AND FOR OURSELVES
        WIN 11, 1 May 1975, p. 9.
        Having no tears like

C-492   EVERYONE SHOULD LIVE
        Fellowship 41, June 1975, pp. 7-8+.

C-493   BERRIGAN: "I DIDN'T DO IT, NED!"
        National Catholic Reporter 11, 20 June 1975, pp. 10-11.

C-494   DANIEL BERRIGAN ON THE MIDDLE EAST
        WIN 11, 24 July 1975, pp. 11-15.

C-495   LEST WE FORGET: AN INTERVIEW WITH DAN BERRIGAN
        Catholic Agitator, September 1975, pp. 1-2.

C-496   LIFE IN THE LABYRINTH
        Catholic Worker, September 1975, pp. 1, 4.

C-497 [LETTER TO THE EDITOR OF *WIN*]
       WIN 11, 18 September 1975, p. 2.

C-498 NO AND YES AND THE WHOLE DAMN THING
       Year One [Baltimore] 1, [November] 1975, pp. 1-2.
       What is the point in saying no, what is the point in
         not saying no?

C-499 GRAVE DIGGING AT THE "BLIGHT HOUSE"
       Fellowship 41, December 1975, p. 18.

C-500 [LETTER TO FRIENDS]
       Year One [Baltimore] 1, Christmas [sic] 1975, p. 1.

                          1976

C-501 SELF-IMMOLATION: A CONVERSATION
       Unmuzzled Ox 4, (1), 1976, pp. 7-15.

C-502 HANDICAPPED
       New Letters 42, Summer 1976, p. 14.
       and the least of these

C-503 WHALE'S TALE
       Katallagete 6, Summer 1976, pp. 24-27.

C-504 *EZRA POUND: THE LAST ROWER, A POLITICAL PROFILE*, BY
         C. DAVID HEYMANN. [review]
       Critic 35, Fall 1976, pp. 76-80.

C-505 FROM A KOREAN PRISON
       Gamaliel 2, Winter 1976, pp. 4-12.

C-506 [IN THE HOUSE WHERE ALL CRY OUT...]
       Fellowship 42, January-February 1976, p. 30.
       In

C-507 A QUESTION OF JUSTICE
       Catholic Worker, February 1976, pp. 1, 3.

C-508 [LETTER TO FRIENDS]
       Year One [Baltimore] 2, March 1976, pp. 1-2.

C-509 LETTER TO THE EDITOR
       Fellowship 42, March 1976, p. 2.

C-510   [LETTER TO THE EDITOR]
        Unity Grapevine [Syracuse, N.Y.], April 1976, p. 3.

C-511   NO AND YES AND THE WHOLE DAMN THING...
        Sojourners 5, April 1976, p. 33.
        What is the point in saying no,

C-512   ALL MANNER OF SIGNS AND WONDERS WILL APPEAR IN THE
            SUN, MOON, AND STARS.
        Fellowship 42, May 1976, pp. 11-13.

C-513   [LETTER TO THE EDITOR]
        Fellowship 42, May 1976, p. 2.

        With Ned Hanauer.

C-514   DELUGE REVISITED
        Israel & Palestine issue 50, 1 July 1976, pp. 10-11.

C-515   200
        National Catholic Reporter, 2 July 1976, p. 9.

C-516   FROM A KOREAN PRISON--A PATH TO LIFE
        Catholic Worker, July-August 1976, pp. 1, 3, 6.

C-517   THE DAY THE EMPIRE FELL: AND HOW AND WHY
        Year One [Baltimore] 2, August 1976, pp. 1-7.

C-518   BLESS THE LORD MY SOUL
        Catholic Worker, December 1976, p. 4.
        We have the catalogue by heart

C-519   CREATE US ANEW
        Catholic Worker, December 1976, p. 5.
        Stronger than we our sins

C-520   EXALTAVIT HUMILES
        Sojourners 5, December 1976, p. 27.
        All things despised, capricious cranky,

C-521   THE FACE OF CHRIST
        Sojourners 5, December 1976, p. 27.
        The tragic beauty of the face of Christ

C-522   GRACE IN THE RUINS
        Sojourners 5, December 1976, p. 27.

        See individual entries for EXALTAVIT HUMILES and THE
        FACE OF CHRIST.

C-523   I LIFT MY EYES TO YOU, MY HELP, MY HOPE: PSALMS AND
             MEDITATIONS
         Catholic Worker, December 1976, pp. 4-5.
         Illustrations by Robert McGovern.

         See individual entries for THEY HAVE IDOLS, A PATHEON
         OF IDOLS; MY HELP, MY HOPE; BLESS THE LORD MY SOUL;
         CREATE US ANEW; WHAT MARVELS THE LORD WORKS FOR THEM;
         I LOVE YOUR PROMISE; SHOW ME YOUR FACE, O GOD.

C-524   I LOVE YOUR PROMISE
         Catholic Worker, December 1976, p. 5.
         A double heart be far from me, Lord

C-525   MY HELP, MY HOPE
         Catholic Worker, December 1976, p. 4.
         I lift my eyes to you

C-526   SHOW ME YOUR FACE, O GOD
         Catholic Worker, December 1976, p. 5.
         At land's end, end of tether

C-527   THEY HAVE IDOLS, A PANTHEON OF IDOLS
         Catholic Worker, December 1976, p. 4.
         Hear the worldlings mock us--

C-528   WHAT MARVELS THE LORD WORKS FOR THEM
         Catholic Worker, December 1976, p. 5.
         When the Spirit struck us free

                              1977

C-529   ZEN POEM FOR DOROTHY DAY
         Cross Currents 28, Spring 1977, pp. 4-6.
         How I long for supernatural powers!

C-530   THE SEVENTY TIMES SEVENTY SEVEN STOREY MOUNTAIN
         Cross Currents 27, Winter 1977-1978, pp. 385-393.

C-531   A MODEST PROPOSAL TO THE COURT
         Year One [Baltimore] 3, February 1977, pp. [1]-4.

C-532   PSALM 73
         Other Side 66, February 1977, [foldout] [unpaginated].
         And

C-533   RESISTANCE
        The Community Church News, February 1977, pp. 1, 4,
        5, 6.

C-534   WHAT DO YOU REALLY BELIEVE ABOUT CHURCH, PEACE AND
        JUSTICE?
        Religion Teacher's Journal 11, March 1977, pp. 37-38.

C-535   BIBLE PARABLES BRISTLE WITH MODERN PAINS--AND HOPES
        HOPES--IN SEABURY BOOK BY BERRIGAN;
        Publishers Weekly, 14 March 1977, p. 72.

        Interview edited by R. Dahlin.

C-536   WHAT ARE WE, THE CHURCH, TO DO?
        National Catholic Reporter, 8 April 1977, pp. 12-13.

C-537   "THEY SAY I AM CRAZY BECAUSE I REFUSE TO BE CRAZY THE
        WAY EVERYBODY ELSE IS CRAZY" [PETER MAURIN: UP-
        STREAM TO THE SOURCE]
        Catholic Worker 43, May 1977, pp. 1, 8, 11.

C-538   LETTER TO LIZ McALISTER (ARLINGTON JAIL, 1977)
        Radix 8, May-June 1977, pp. 5-6.
        Opening your letters and Phil's is like taking the
        sacrament

C-539   FROM A KOREAN PRISON--A PATH TO LIFE
        Friends Journal 23, 15 June 1977, pp. 357-362.

C-540   HOMECOMING
        Christian Century 94, July 1977, p. 655.
        I came in from jail

C-541   THE RUSSIAN PRISONER
        Christian Century 94, July 1977, p. 656.
        Veteran of psychiatric jungles

C-542   STAR WARS: CRUEL FANTASY
        Sojourners 6, September 1977, pp. 32-34.

C-543   MODESTY IN IMMODEST TIMES
        Unity, October 1977, pp. 1, 11.

C-544   LETTER TO LIZ McALISTER (ARLINGTON JAIL, 1977)
        WIN 13, 10 November 1977, pp. 16-17.
        Opening your letters and Phil's is like taking the
        sacrament

C-545 THE FEAST OF CARRION
       Year One [Baltimore] 3, December 1977, pp. 7-11.

C-546 THE WHALE'S TALE
       Catholic Worker, December 1977, pp. 4-5.

       Art by Robert Hodgell and Robert McGovern.

C-547 THE LEVELING OF JOHN McNEILL: SILENCING A MAN AND A
          BOOK
       Commonweal 104, 9 December 1977, pp. 778-783.

C-548 DOOMSDAY BOY THE TINKER TOY, OR THE NEUTRON IN THE
          NURSERY (a meditation for adults)
       WIN 13, 22 December 1977, pp. 8-9.
       Doomsday boy comes life size, a wooden child on wheels.
          It speaks, runs,

D

PHILIP BERRIGAN
Books

D-1 NO MORE STRANGERS. New York: Macmillan, 1965.

Essays. 12 April 1965. 181 pp. 22 cm. Dust jacket: white
and brown lettering on black background by Stan Phillips.
Publication figures not available. Paperback edition published by Divine Word. (Material previously published in *Perspectives*, the *Catholic Worker*, *Worship*, *New City*, *Crosslight*,
and *Continuum*. Dedicated to the author's brother, Daniel.)

Contents:

a   INTRODUCTION BY THOMAS MERTON, pp. xi-xx.
b   1. THE NATURE OF CHRISTIAN WITNESS, pp. 1-30.
c   2. CHRIST AND THE SHAPE OF MANKIND, pp. 31-48.
d   3. WITH MY BODY, I WORSHIP YOU, pp. 49-74.
e   4. RACIAL PATTERNS AND THE CHRISTIAN, pp. 75-104.
f   5. SEGREGATION AND THE NUCLEAR ARMS RACE, pp. 105-132.
g   6. RACE AND THE CHRISTIAN CONSCIENCE, pp. 133-158.
h   7. THE CHURCH AND THE WORLD, pp. 159-181.

D-2 A PUNISHMENT FOR PEACE. New York: Macmillan, 1969.

Essays. 26 May 1969. 178 pp. 22 cm. Dust jacket: orange
design, white and gray lettering on black background by Bob
Cuevas. Publication figures not available. (Dedicated to
the parents of the author and the Catonsville Nine.)

Contents:

a   1. CONSENSUS SOCIETY! CONSENSUS CHURCH?, pp. 1-26.
b   2. THE COLOR OF POVERTY, pp. 27-56.
c   3. THE FIRE THIS TIME?, pp. 57-82.

d 4. IMPERIALISM, THE GOLDEN RULE OF PEACE, pp. 83-111.
e 5. COLD-WAR ASPIRATIONS AND SECRETS, pp. 112-144.
f 6. REFLECTIONS ON CHURCH-STATE COVENANTS, pp. 145-169.
g [PRESS STATEMENT OF THE BALTIMORE 4], pp. 145-147.
h EPILOGUE. [PRESS STATEMENT OF THE CATONSVILLE 9], pp.
     171-174.

D-3 PRISON JOURNALS OF A PRIEST REVOLUTIONARY. Compiled and
edited by Vincent McGee. New York: Holt, Rinehart and Winston, 1970.

Essays, journal, and conversations. 15 June 1970. 198 pp.
22 cm. Dust jacket: black and white design with orange and
brown lettering on white background by Fred Gerlach and Ate-
lier West. Photograph of author on back. Publication figures
not available. Paperback edition published by Ballantine.
(Dedicated to Thomas Merton, David Darst, and others.)

Contents:

a EDITOR'S NOTE BY VINCENT McGEE, pp. ix-x.
b THE BREAKING OF MEN AND THE BREAKING OF BREAD: AN INTRO-
     DUCTION BY DANIEL BERRIGAN, pp. xi-xix.
c [AUTHOR'S NOTE], pp. xxi-xxii.
d CAN WE SERVE BOTH LOVE AND WAR?, pp. 1-7.
e STATEMENT AT SENTENCING, MAY 24, 1968, pp. 8-13.
f LETTER FROM A BALTIMORE JAIL, pp. 14-20.
g A COMMUNITY OF NINE, pp. 21-26.
h A DAY IN THE PEN: AN INTERVIEW, pp. 27-57.
i PRISON JOURNAL, 1968, pp. 58-110.
j THE TRIAL, pp. 111-137.
k STATEMENT AT SENTENCING, NOVEMBER 8, 1968, pp. 138-143.
l PRISON JOURNAL, CONTINUED, pp. 144-181.
m A PRIEST IN THE RESISTANCE: AN INTERVIEW, pp. 182-198.

D-4 WIDEN THE PRISON GATES: Writing from Jails April 1970-
December 1972. New York: Simon & Schuster, 1973.

Journal. 20 November 1973. 261 pp. 22 cm. Dust jacket:
color photograph of author with white lettering by Lawrence
Ratzkin. Publication figures not available. Paperback edition published by Touchstone. (Dedicated to Carol, Jerry,
and Daniel Berrigan and others. One section previously published in *WIN*.)

Contents:

D-5 OF BEASTS AND BEASTLY IMAGES: Essays under the BOMB.
Portland, Ore.: Sunburst Press, 1979.

Essays. 27 April 1979. 90 pp. 21 cm. Cover design: orange
and white illustration by George Knowlton, orange lettering
on white background. Photograph of author by unidentified
photographer on back. Published in soft cover only. Illustrations by George Knowlton. Publication figures not available. (Some material previously published in *WIN*, *Katallagete*,
and *Year One* [Baltimore]. Dedicated to the author's wife,
Elizabeth McAlister.)

Contents:

E

PHILIP BERRIGAN
Contributions to Books by Other Authors

1967

E-1 [INTERVIEW WITH JAMES FINN] in James Finn (editor).
Protest: Pacifism and Politics. New York: Random
House, 1967. Pp. 72-83.

1968

E-2 BLOOD, WAR AND WITNESS in John O'Connor (editor).
American Catholic Exodus. Washington [D.C.]: Corpus
Books, 1968. Pp. 5-23.

1972

E-3 PROLOGUE [excerpt from NO MORE STRANGERS] in Stephen Halpert and Tom Murray (editors). *Witness of the Berrigans*.
Garden City, N.Y.: Doubleday, 1972. P. 13.

1973

E-4 FOREWORD in Daniel Berrigan. *Prison Poems*. Greensboro,
N.C.: Unicorn Press, 1973. Unpaginated.

E-5 AN OPEN LETTER TO A BISHOP in Edward Guinan (editor).
     Peace and Nonviolence. New York: Paulist Press, 1973.
     Pp. 17-24.

                              1977

E-6 FOREWORD in Joseph Mulligan. *Liberation For the Poor of
     Yahweh* [,] *Pharaohs* [,] *And Christians*. Portland, Ore.:
     Sunburst, 1977. Pp. vii-xiii.

F

PHILIP BERRIGAN
Contributions to Periodicals

1957

F-1   A PARISH APOSTOLATE
       Worship 31, October 1957, pp. 553-558.

1960

F-2   THE CHALLENGE OF SEGREGATION
       Worship 34, November 1960, pp. 597-604.

1961

F-3   THE CHALLENGE OF SEGREGATION
       Interracial Review 34, February 1961, pp. 30-31+.

F-4   THE RACE PROBLEM AND THE CHRISTIAN CONSCIENCE
       Catholic Worker, December 1961, pp. 1, 4-8.

1962

F-5   A HOPEFUL SIGN OF RENEWAL
       Josephite Harvest 74, January 1962, pp. 17-19.

F-6   LIVING THE MYSTERY OF MARRIAGE
        Worship 36, July 1962, pp. 437-444.

                              1963

F-7   SEGREGATION AND THE NUCLEAR ARMS RACE
        Crosslight 4, 1963, pp. 170-182.

F-8   THE LITURGY AND SEGREGATION
        Center 5, Fall 1963, pp. 5-19.

F-9   POSTSCRIPT TO THE MARCH ON WASHINGTON
        Continuum 1, Autumn 1963, pp. 406-408.

        Co-authored with Daniel Berrigan.

F-10   CHRIST AND THE SHAPE OF MANKIND
        Catholic Worker 29, May 1963, pp. 2, 7, 8.

        Co-authored with Daniel Berrigan.

F-11   CATHOLIC CHURCH AND THE NEGRO
        Divine Word Messenger 40, July 1963, pp. 154-155, 158.

F-12   CATHOLIC CHURCH AND THE NEGRO [REPLY TO ROBERT SENSER]
        Perspectives 8, July-August 1963, p. 121.

F-13   RACIAL MARCH MOVING EXPERIENCE
        Syracuse *Post-Standard*, 8 September 1963, p. 6.

        Co-authored with Daniel Berrigan.

F-14   LAY LEADERS IN ACTION
        Josephite Harvest 75, September-October 1963, pp. 18-21.

                              1964

F-15   RACISM AND ROMAN CATHOLICS
        Continuum 1, Winter 1964, pp. 516-522.

        Co-authored with Daniel Berrigan.

F-16   THE LITURGY AND THE RACIAL STRUGGLE
        Catholic Worker, May 1964, pp. 4, 11.

F-17 CHRISTIAN WITNESS TODAY
      Perspectives 9, July-August 1964, pp. 102-109.

F-18 RACIAL PATTERNS AND THE CHRISTIAN
      New City 3, October 1964, pp. 22-26.

F-19 CHRISTIANITY IN HARLEM
      Commonweal 81, 27 November 1964, pp. 323-325.

                         1965

F-20 THE PROPHETIC MINISTRY
      Continuum 3, Summer 1965, pp. 252-254.

      Co-authored with Daniel Berrigan.

F-21 DECLARATION OF CONSCIENCE
      Catholic Worker, February 1965, p. 2.

      Co-signed with Daniel Berrigan.

F-22 THE BLACK MAN'S BURDEN
      Catholic Worker, April 1965, pp. 1, 7-8.

F-23 RACE AND CONSCIENCE
      National Catholic Reporter, 28 April 1965.

F-24 VIETNAM AND AMERICA'S CONSCIENCE
      Catholic Worker, October 1965, pp. 2, 6.

                         1966

F-25 THE ONE HUNDRED CONVOCATIONS OF THE F.O.R.
      Continuum 3, Winter 1966, pp. 513-515.

F-26 THE PRIEST AND SOCIETY
      Ave Maria 103, 8 January 1966, p. 19.

F-27 CATHOLIC PRIEST SAYS VIETNAM WAR DESTROYS HUMAN VALUES
      Gazette and Daily, [York, Pa.] 25 July 1966, p. 17.

      Address at Gettysburg.

F-28   [PACIFISM]
       Sign 46, August 1966, p. 17.

F-29   THE PATHOLOGY OF RACISM
       Catholic Worker, October-November 1966, pp. 1, 5.

                              1967

F-30   PRISON NOTES
       Catholic Worker, November 1967, pp. 1, 6.

F-31   THE UNITED STATES AND REVOLUTION--WHAT PATH WILL AMERI-
          CANS FOLLOW?
       Worldview 10, November 1967, pp. 10-13.

F-32   MUSINGS FROM BALTIMORE CITY JAIL
       Commonweal 87, 7 November 1967, pp. 195-196.

F-33   "END THE WAR" MESSAGE IS SENT TO VIETS BY BERRIGANS
       Catholic Messenger, 30 November 1967, p. 12.

F-34   WE SHED OUR BLOOD WILLINGLY
       Catholic Peace Fellowship Bulletin, December 1967, p. 2.

       Baltimore 4 statement.

F-35   FACT AND FANCIES FROM PRISON
       Christianity and Crisis 27, 11 December 1967, pp. 292-
          293.

       Letter from Baltimore Jail.

                              1968

F-36   INCARNATION AND WAR
       Katallagete [1], Spring 1968, pp. 24-27.

F-37   HELL IS OTHER PEOPLE
       Continuum 6, Fall 1968, pp. 414-417.

F-38   THE LAST SUNDAY AFTER PENTECOST
       Katallagete 2, Winter 1968-1969, pp. 26-28.

F-39   CONVERSATIONS ON REVOLUTION
      National Catholic Reporter, 28 February 1968, p. 5.

      1st in a series of 4 articles.

F-40   CONVERSATIONS ON REVOLUTION
      National Catholic Reporter, 6 March 1968, pp. 6-7.

      2nd in a series of 4 articles.

F-41   CONVERSATIONS ON REVOLUTION
      National Catholic Reporter, 20 March 1968, pp. 8-9.

      3rd in a series of 4 articles.

F-42   U.S. POLICY AND REVOLUTION
      Catholic Peace Fellowship Bulletin, April 1968, pp. 4-6.

F-43   CONVERSATIONS ON REVOLUTION
      National Catholic Reporter, 10 April 1968, p. 6.

      4th in a series of 4 articles.

F-44   WHY WE BURN DRAFT RECORDS
      National Catholic Reporter, 29 May 1968, p. 6.

F-45   ON JAIL COMMUNITY
      Catholic Peace Fellowship Bulletin, June 1968, pp. 3-4,
         15.

F-46   THE BERRIGAN CASE
      Commonweal 88, 14 June 1968, p. 373.

      Excerpt from statement prior to court sentence, Balti-
      more 4.

F-47   NAPALMING DRAFT FILES--A LETTER FROM JAIL
      Liberation 13, July-August 1968, pp. 20-21.

F-48   LETTER FROM A BALTIMORE JAIL
      Christianity and Crisis 28, 22 July 1968, pp. 168-170.

F-49   VIOLENCE: A PRISONER'S VIEW
      Christian Century 85, 13 August 1968, pp. 1011-1013.

F-50   INCARNATION AND WAR
      Catholic Worker, September 1968, pp. 5-6.

F-51   STATEMENT AT SENTENCING
      National Catholic Reporter, 20 November 1968, p. 4.

Individual statements by members of the Catonsville
Nine.

F-52   STATEMENT AT SENTENCING
       Christian Century 85, 4 December 1968, pp. 1539-1540.

1969

F-53   BERRIGAN: DIALOGUE WITH DOUBT
       Liberation 13, February 1969, pp. 18-25.

F-54   LETTER TO RADICAL CATHOLICS
       Playboy 16, February 1969, pp. 54-55.

F-55   AN APOLOGIA FOR CAT
       Year One [Ithaca, N.Y.] 3, December 1969--January
          1970, pp. 39-47.

1970

F-56   TEXT OF BERRIGANS' PRISON SERMON
       National Catholic Reporter, 20 November 1970, p. 12.

       Co-authored with Daniel Berrigan.

1971

F-57   LETTER FROM PRISON
       Catholic Agitator, January 1971, pp. 3, 8.

F-58   LETTERS FROM BERRIGAN CASE
       New York *Times*, 1 May 1971, p. 12.

F-59   CLARIFICATION OF REVOLUTION, BERRIGAN STYLE
       Los Angeles *News Advocate*, 20 August-15 September 1971,
          p. 11.

1972

F-60   PHILIP'S BANNED SPEECH
       Catonsville Roadrunner, issue 34, Spring 1972, p. 16.

F-61   A PRIEST IN RESISTANCE
       Catholic Worker, February 1972, pp. 1, 3, 8.

F-62   PHILIP BERRIGAN: WHAT THE JURY WON'T HEAR
       Harrisburg *Independent Press*, 2-8 March 1972, p. 5.

F-63   OPEN LETTER TO A BISHOP
       Commonweal 96, 26 May 1972, pp. 282-285.

       1st of 2 articles.

F-64   OPEN LETTER TO A BISHOP
       Commonweal 96, 28 July 1972, p. 395.

       2nd of 2 articles.

F-65   A STATEMENT OF HOPE
       Harrisburg *Independent Press*, 15-22 September 1972,
          pp. 4, 2 [sic].
       Statement before sentencing, Harrisburg 7.

F-66   I WOULD RATHER TALK ABOUT HOPE
       Commonweal 96, 29 September 1972, pp. 516-517.

       Excerpt from statement at sentencing, 5 September 1972.

F-67   "I WOULD RATHER TALK ABOUT HOPE"
       Catholic Worker, October-November 1972, p. 3.

F-68   SHARING OUR LIVES WITH THE INDOCHINESE
       Village Voice, 23 November 1972, pp. 12-14.

F-69   LETTER FROM PRISON BUILDING
       Syracuse Peace Council, December 1972, pp. 18-19.

F-70   A CHRISTMAS PRAYER
       New York *Times* [Week in Review], December 24, 1972, p. 9.

1973

F-71   PRISONS AND WAR.   EXCERPTS FROM THE STATEMENT OF FR.
          PHILIP BERRIGAN UPON HIS RELEASE FROM PRISON
          Fellowship 39, January 1973, p. 12.

F-72   PHIL BERRIGAN ON THE TRIAL
          WIN 9, 15 March 1973, pp. 32-41.

F-73   TEXT OF THE BERRIGAN-McALISTER STATEMENT
          National Catholic Reporter, 8 June 1973, p. 21.

          Co-authored with Elizabeth McAlister.

F-74   ON THE TORTURE OF PRISONERS
          Fellowship 39, September 1973, pp. 4-5.

F-75   ON THE TORTURE OF PRISONERS
          WIN 9, 6 September 1973, pp. 16-17.

F-76   THE HEROIC IDOL AND THE SLOUCHING BEAST
          Peace News, 16 November 1973, p. 5.
          ON THE TORTURE OF PRISONERS--fragment.

1974

F-77   THE INSTITUTION AND ANARCHISM: BERRIGAN INTERVIEW
          Catonsville Roadrunner, issue 35, Spring 1974, p. 5.

F-78   OF POISONS AND ANTIDOTES
          Katallagete 5, Winter 1974, pp. 8-11.

F-79   ARNOLD'S VICTORY
          WIN 10, 18 April 1974, pp. 14-15.

F-80   AN INTERVIEW WITH PHILIP BERRIGAN
          Catholic Agitator, June 1974, pp. 1-2.

F-81   ON KINGMAKING
          WIN 10, 18 July 1974, pp. 12-14.

F-82   AN INTERVIEW WITH PHILIP BERRIGAN
          Right On 6, October 1974, pp. 1, 8.

F-83   TWO PRISONERS
       WIN 10, 19 December 1974, pp. 17-19.

                              1975

F-84   NEITHER VICTIMS NOR EXECUTIONERS
       Quotha [SUNY, Binghamton], 5 February 1975, pp. 7-10.

F-85   THE COLLAPSE OF AMERICA'S INDOCHINA EMPIRE
       WIN 11, 1 May 1975, pp. 7-8.

F-86   COMMUNITY IN THE MIDST OF VIOLENCE
       Vanguard, May-June 1975, pp. 12-13.

       Interview with Philip Berrigan by Carol Ricker Wilson
       and Peter Reitsma.

F-87   [NOTHING HAS CHANGED]
       Fellowship 41, June 1975, p. 6.

F-88   THE PROPHET AS SENTRY / SHEPHERD
       In the Tracks of the Dinosaur, June 1975, pp. 1, 4.

F-89   IN THE WAKE OF WAR: NO LESSONS, JUST CORPSES
       Harrisburg *Independent Press*, 22 August - 5 September
          1975, pp. 4, 6.

F-90   NOTHING HAS CHANGED
       Catholic Agitator, September 1975, pp. 2-3.

F-91   ON AMERICAN BUYING AND SELLING, OR (IF THE BUCK MOVES
          YOU, PASS IT)
       Year One [Baltimore] 1, Christmas [sic] 1975, pp. 4-7.

                              1976

F-92   SPIRITUAL SLAVERY, CONSCIENTIOUS ACTS
       Catholic Agitator, January 1976, pp. 4-5.

F-93   PHIL BERRIGAN'S CONSCIENTIOUS OBJECTIONS TO LAW
       National Catholic Reporter, 16 April 1976, p. 11.

F-94   AMERICA'S AFFAIR WITH THE BOMB, OR SPECULATIONS ON
        DEICIDE
        Year One [Baltimore] 2, August 1976, pp. 7-10.

F-95   ANARCHY AND THE SUMMER CAMPAIGN
        Year One [Baltimore] 2, October 1976, pp. 1-2.

F-96   CONCERNING THANKSGIVING--AMERIKAN OR REAL?
        Year One [Baltimore] 2, December 1976, pp. 14-16.

                                    1977

F-97   AN INTERVIEW WITH LIZ McALLISTER [sic], PHIL BERRIGAN,
        DAN BERRIGAN
        Sojourners 6, February 1977, pp. 22-26.
        [STRENGTHEN ALL FEEBLE ARMS, STEADY ALL TOTTERING KNEES]

F-98   PHIL BERRIGAN'S STATEMENT PRIOR TO SENTENCING, JAN. 31,
        1977
        Year One [Baltimore] 3, February 1977, pp. 4-5.

F-99   ANOTHER HELPER---ANOTHER BEAST
        Year One [Baltimore] 3, July 1977, pp. 1-3.

G

ELIZABETH McALISTER BERRIGAN
Contributions to Periodicals

1971

G-1   SISTER ELIZABETH McALISTER: AN INTERVIEW
      Commonweal 95, 15 October 1971, pp. 63-66.

1972

G-2   LETTERS FROM BERRIGAN CASE
      New York *Times* [Week in Review], 2 May 1972, p. 10.

1973

G-3   TEXT OF THE BERRIGAN-McALISTER STATEMENT
      National Catholic Reporter, 8 June 1973, p. 21.

G-4   SOIL FOR SOCIAL CHANGE
      Theology Today 30, October 1973, pp. 239-242.

1974

G-5   FORMING COMMUNITY: BALTIMORE'S JONAH HOUSE
      Fellowship 40, February 1974, pp. 5-6.

G-6   SOME REFLECTIONS ON THE MEANING OF RESISTANCE ACTION
       TODAY
       WIN 10, 23 May 1974, pp. 13-15.

G-7   FEMINISTS FOR LIFE?
       WIN 10, 4 July 1974, pp. 8-9.

G-8   REVIEW OF *CONSPIRACY: THE IMPLICATIONS OF THE HARRIS-
       BURG TRIAL*
       Fellowship 40, November 1974, p. 20.

                                 1975

G-9   VIETNAM: A CASE FOR REMEMBERING
       Harrisburg *Independent Press*, 23-30 May 1975, p. 7.

                                 1976

G-10   THE PRICE OF MAKING PEACE
       Catholic Agitator, March 1976, p. 3.

G-11   PROPOSAL FOR A NATIONAL DEBATE ON NUCLEAR POLICY
       Year One [Baltimore] 2, March 1976, pp. 2-3.

G-12   CONTEMPLATIVE ACTION
       Catholic Agitator, September 1976, p. 3.

G-13   INEVITABLE DESTRUCTION OR NEW POSSIBILITIES
       Year One [Baltimore] 2, December 1976, pp. 10-14.

                                 1977

G-14   LIZ McALISTER'S STATEMENT PRIOR TO RESENTENCING--
       JANUARY 24, 1977
       Year One [Baltimore] 3, February 1977, pp. 10-11.

G-15   AN INTERVIEW WITH LIZ McALLISTER [sic], PHIL BERRIGAN,
       DAN BERRIGAN
       Sojourners 6, February 1977, pp. 22-26.

G-16 [MESSAGE FROM JAIL IN ALEXANDRIA, VA.]
    Year One [Baltimore] 3, May 1977, pp. 6-7.

G-17 A PRISON LETTER: RAISING CHILDREN, RESISTANCE,
    COMMUNITY
    Radix 8, May-June 1977, pp. 3-7.

    Photos by Ched Myers.

G-18 ASKING CARTER TO TAKE HIS FAITH SERIOUSLY
    Year One [Baltimore] 3, December 1977, pp. 11-12.

H

THE BERRIGANS: A SELECTIVE BIBLIOGRAPHY

1958

H-1   Coffey, Thomas.   A NEW LIGHT IN CATHOLIC LETTERS.
      Spiritual Life 4, March 1958, pp. 9-14.

      Daniel Berrigan's first collection of poetry, TIME
      WITHOUT NUMBER, is seen as an example of a new Catholic
      humanism.

1963

H-2   De Leon, Shirley.   NUCLEAR PACIFIST.   *Today* 18, March
      1963, pp. 3-5.

      The author discusses Daniel Berrigan's call for an ecu-
      menical movement devoted to the solution of human
      problems.

1964

H-3   Sister M. Therese.   POET AT GEORGETOWN.   (DANIEL BERRI-
      GAN, S.J.).   *Catholic Worker*, December 1964, p. 6.

      Poem about Daniel Berrigan.

1965

H-4   Berrigan, Jerome C.   SYRACUSE TO MONTGOMERY--AND BACK.
        Catholic Sun [Syracuse, N.Y.], 8 April 1965, p. 3.

        Jerome Charles Berrigan, brother of Daniel and Philip,
        reports on his trip with 43 others from Syracuse to a
        massive civil rights demonstration in Montgomery, Ala-
        bama, led by Martin Luther King, Jr.

H-5   Institute for Freedom in the Church.   OPEN LETTER TO
        THE AUTHORITIES OF THE ARCHDIOCESE OF NEW YORK AND THE
        JESUIT COMMUNITY IN NEW YORK CITY.   New York *Times*, 12
        December 1965, p. 4.

        One-page advertisement demanding the return of Daniel
        Berrigan from his Latin American "exile" and asking
        that he not be silenced by the church.

1966

H-6   THE "SILENCED" PRIESTS--A SPECIAL ISSUE.   *Ave Maria* 103,
        8 January 1966.

        Contains case histories of silenced priests including
        Daniel Berrigan, Gommar De Pauw, Maurice Ouellet,
        Philip Berrigan, John Coffield, William Du Bay.   Also
        features Philip Berrigan's article THE PRIEST AND SO-
        CIETY, and a special study of religious obedience.

H-7   Cameron, J.M.   WHAT IS A CHRISTIAN?   *New York Review of
        Books*, 26 May 1966, pp. 3-4.

        Review of three recent religious books including Daniel
        Berrigan's THEY CALL US DEAD MEN.   Sees Berrigan favor-
        ably as a "universal Catholic" who presents a radical
        challenge to "middle-class" Catholicism.

1967

H-8   Finn, James (editor).   PROTEST: PACIFISM AND POLITICS.
        New York: Random House, 1967.

Interviews peace activists, including Daniel and Philip Berrigan, and their associates in the Catholic Worker movement and the Catholic Peace Fellowship.

H-9   Hinckle, Warren. LEFT WING CATHOLICS. *Ramparts* 6, November 1967, pp. 14-26.

Vignettes of leading Catholic "dissidents," including the Berrigans, William Du Bay, James Groppi, and Fulton J. Sheen.

1968

H-10 Douglass, James W. THE NON-VIOLENT CROSS: A THEOLOGY OF REVOLUTION AND PEACE. New York: Macmillan, 1968.

A theology for nonviolent revolution, written by a close friend of Dorothy Day, Thomas Merton, and Daniel and Philip Berrigan. Douglass acknowledges both Berrigans for help with the book.

H-11 Merton, Thomas. FAITH AND VIOLENCE: CHRISTIAN TEACHING AND CHRISTIAN PRACTICE. Notre Dame, Ind.: University of Notre Dame, 1968.

A collection of essays on peace-related issues by the well known Trappist writer, Thomas Merton. The book is dedicated to James Forest, a member of the Milwaukee 14, and Philip Berrigan.

H-12 Torrens, James. BERRIGAN IN HIS POEMS. *Good Work* 31, Fall 1968, pp. 115-119.

A brief analysis of Daniel Berrigan's collected poems.

H-13 Cornell, Tom [Thomas Charles]. NONVIOLENT NAPALM IN CATONSVILLE. *Catholic Worker*, June 1968, pp. 1-2, 8.

A Catholic pacifist looks at the shift toward revolutionary tactics in the antiwar movement as evidenced by the Berrigan-led draft board raid at Catonsville.

H-14 Ruether, Rosemary. RUETHER'S OPEN LETTER TO DANIEL BERRIGAN. *National Catholic Reporter*, 5 June 1968, p. 4.

A theologian critically evaluates symbolic gestures as political action in a letter to Daniel Berrigan.

H-15 Ruether, Rosemary. TACTICS FAIL THE VISION. *National Catholic Reporter*, 26 June 1968, p. 4.

Ruether takes issue with Daniel Berrigan's letter in *NCR*'s 19 June 1968 issue.

H-16 Merton, Thomas. DOES NAPALM REALLY COMMUNICATE. *Ave Maria* 108, 7 September 1968, pp. 9-10.

Merton writes of his continued faith in nonviolence, and views the actions of the Catonsville 9 as prophetic nonviolent provocation.

H-17 Deming, Barbara. TRIAL BY AUTOPSY (CATONSVILLE 9 VS. JUDGE THOMSEN). *Liberation* 13, December 1968, pp. 6-11.

A political activist, sympathetic to the Berrigans, on the federal proceedings against the Catonsville 9.

1969

H-18 Cargas, Harry J. DANIEL BERRIGAN: THE ACTIVIST AS POET. *Laurel Review* 9, Spring 1969, pp. 11-17.

Desultory paper evaluating Daniel Berrigan's early major writings as indicative of the future direction of his life.

H-19 Lewis, Tom. THE ARTIST AS PROPHETIC ACTIVIST. *Motive* 29, February 1969, p. 39.

An artist member of the Baltimore 4 and Catonsville 9, and close associate of Daniel and Philip Berrigan, discusses his views on art and life. Lewis illustrated TRIAL POEMS by Daniel Berrigan.

H-20 Lewis, W. Jack. SOAP BOX [column], *Fortnight* [Cornell University], 14 May 1969, pp. F2, F4.

The Director of Cornell United Religious Work discusses the reorganization of CURW, the religious service organization with which Daniel Berrigan was associated during his stay at Cornell University.

H-21 Gray, Francine du Plessix. THE ULTRA-RESISTANCE. *New York Review of Books*, 25 September 1969, pp. 11-22.

A journalist interprets the Milwaukee 14 action as
part of a larger movement inspired by Daniel and Philip
Berrigan.

1970

H-22 Gray, Francine du Plessix. DIVINE DISOBEDIENCE. New
      York: Alfred A. Knopf, 1970.

      Largely based on a series done for the *New Yorker*,
      these portraits of Emmaus House (New York City), the
      Berrigans, Mendez Arceo, and Ivan Illich illumine dif-
      ferent aspects of the "Catholic Left."

H-23 Gray, Francine du Plessix. PROFILES. *New Yorker* 46,
      14 March 1970, pp. 44-46+.

      To date, the best published biographical work on the
      Berrigans, written by a journalist and novelist.

H-24 Fitch, Bob [Robert Beck]. FORTY-EIGHT HOURS WITH THE
      BERRIGANS. *Christian Century* 87, 20 May 1970, pp. 643-646.

      A photographer writes of Daniel and Philip Berrigan.

H-25 Horowitz, Jack. CATONSVILLE 9 GO UNDERGROUND. *WIN* 6,
      1 June 1970, pp. 14-16.

      Focuses on Cornell University's Freedom Seder in April
      1970, and Daniel Berrigan's appearance there.

H-26 Nobile, Philip. THE PRIEST WHO STAYED OUT IN THE COLD.
      New York *Times Magazine*, 28 June 1970, pp. 8-9, 38, 40,
      43-44, 50.

      Philip Nobile meets with Daniel Berrigan underground
      and they discuss such topics as resistance, liberation,
      and the nuclear family.

H-27 Moylan, Mary. [LETTER]. *Catonsville Roadrunner*, issue
      16, July 1970, unpaginated.

      A member of the Catonsville 9, who went underground,
      discusses her reasons for refusing to serve her prison
      sentence.

H-28 Nobile, Philip and Francine du Plessix Gray. DROPOUTS
      FORFEIT "RADICAL" BADGES. *National Catholic Reporter*,
      21 August 1970, pp. 12-13.

Nobile interviews Francine du Plessix Gray concerning her book DIVINE DISOBEDIENCE.

H-29 Ruether, Rosemary. THE DISCUSSION CONTINUES. *Commonweal* 32, 4 September 1970, p. 431.

Ruether comments on Daniel Berrigan's HOW TO MAKE A DIFFERENCE and questions the validity of his charismatic leadership.

H-30 Fitch, Bob [Robert Beck]. BERRIGAN: A PHOTO ESSAY. *Motive* 31, November 1970, pp. 9-19.

Photographs of Daniel Berrigan taken while underground in 1970.

H-31 Nobile, Philip. SENATOR GOODELL AND PHILIP BERRIGAN: AN UNTOLD STORY. *New York Review of Books*, 5 November 1970, pp. 38-40.

An account of Philip Berrigan's incarceration at Lewisburg Prison and Senator Charles Goodell's efforts at helping Berrigan obtain a transfer from that institution.

H-32 Day, Dorothy. DAN BERRIGAN IN ROCHESTER. *Catholic Worker*, December 1970, pp. 1, 6.

An account of Daniel Berrigan's treatment by federal authorities while traveling between Danbury Federal Penitentiary and the "Flower City Conspiracy" trial in Rochester, New York.

H-33 Anderson, William R. [REMARKS ON THE BERRIGANS]. *Congressional Record* [House of Representatives], 9 December 1970, pp. H11441-H11444.

Friendly view of the East Coast Conspiracy by Tennessee Representative William R. Anderson.

1971

H-34 Ferber, Michael, and Staughton Lynd. THE RESISTANCE. Boston: Beacon Press, 1971.

Two activists, one a historian, trace the development of the Resistance to the Vietnam War in the United States. The work provides a historical context for the Berrigans' acts of resistance. See especially "The Ultra-Resistance."

H-35 Fitch, Bob [Robert Beck]. MY EYES HAVE SEEN. San Francisco: Glide Publications, 1971.

A largely photographic account of American nonviolent movements of the sixties; includes some photographs of Daniel and Philip Berrigan while underground in 1970.

H-36 Hitchcock, James. THE DECLINE AND FALL OF RADICAL CATHOLICISM. New York: Herder and Herder, 1971.

A study of American Catholicism in the sixties, which confuses liberal and radical religion, but which attempts to explain main currents in post-Vatican II American Catholic thinking. Sees Daniel Berrigan as acting out of "a religious sense."

H-37 Melville, Thomas and Marjorie. WHOSE HEAVEN, WHOSE EARTH? New York: Alfred A. Knopf, 1971.

Former Maryknoll missionaries and members of the Catonsville 9 discuss their lives and commitments.

H-38 Riemer, George (editor). THE NEW JESUITS. Boston: Little, Brown, 1971.

Riemer interviews contemporary Jesuits, including Daniel Berrigan. Brief essay by Riemer on Jesuit life.

H-39 Stringfellow, William, and Anthony Towne. SUSPECT TENDERNESS: THE ETHICS OF THE BERRIGAN WITNESS. New York: Holt, Rinehart and Winston, 1971.

Two friends of Daniel Berrigan, later charged with harboring him as a fugitive from justice, discuss Daniel Berrigan's resistance in the context of Christian theology and ethics.

H-40 Ludwig, Robert A. THE THEOLOGY OF DANIEL BERRIGAN. *Listening* 6, Spring 1971, pp. 127-137.

Points to free choice as a major contribution of Daniel Berrigan's new theology.

H-41 Casey, William Van Etten (editor). THE BURDEN OF THE BERRIGANS. Reprint of *Holy Cross Quarterly* 4, January 1971.

Contents:

a Casey, William Van Etten, S.J. EDITORIAL, p. 3.
b Duff, Edward, S.J. THE BURDEN OF THE BERRIGANS,
      pp. 4-12.
c Clifford, Richard, S.J. THE BERRIGANS--PROPHETIC?,
      pp. 14, 16, 18.
d Greeley, Andrew. [THE BERRIGANS--] PHRENETIC?, pp.
      7, 15, 19.
e Chomsky, Noam. ON THE LIMITS OF CIVIL DISOBEDIENCE,
      pp. 22-31.
f Nobile, Philip. PHIL BERRIGAN IN PRISON, pp. 32-38.
g Brown, Robert McAfee. THE BERRIGANS: SIGNS OR
      MODELS?, pp. 40-48.
h O'Brien, David J. THE BERRIGANS AND AMERICA, pp.
      52-58.
i Gray, Francine du Plessix, et al. PHIL BERRIGAN IN
      HAWAII, pp. 60-64.
j Raines, John C. THE FOLLOWERS OF LIFE, pp. 65-69.
k Hoover, J. Edgar, et al. HOOVER AND THE BERRIGANS,
      pp. 70-80. Documents relating to conspiracy char-
      ges against the Berrigans.

NOTE: THE BURDEN OF THE BERRIGANS was printed in an
expanded edition, THE BERRIGANS, New York: Avon Books,
June 1971. [THE BERRIGANS--] PHRENETIC? by Andrew
Greeley (H-41-d) was not included in this version because Greeley refused to grant permission for a reprint.

New in the anthology are:

xa Ruether, Rosemary Radford. BEYOND CONFRONTATION: THE
      THERAPEUTIC TASK, pp. 113-120.
xb Forest, Jim. PHILIP BERRIGAN: DISTURBER OF SLEEP,
      pp. 166-179.
xc Cowan, Paul. FATHER DAN BERRIGAN: FUGITIVE FROM
      INJUSTICE, pp. 180-190.
xd "Four Families." DAN BERRIGAN WITH FAMILIES IN THE
      UNDERGROUND, pp. 191-202.
xe Coles, Robert. THINKING ABOUT THOSE PRIESTS, pp.
      214-219.

Also included is a reprint of Daniel Berrigan's LETTER
TO THE WEATHERMEN, pp. 203-213.

H-42 THE BERRIGANS: CONSPIRACY AND CONSCIENCE. *Time*, 25
      January 1971, pp. 12-17.

      A feature article on the Berrigans and the government
      charges against them in the Kissinger kidnapping plot.

H-43 Potter, Ray. JEROME BERRIGAN CARRIES IT ON FOR HIS IMPRISONED BROTHERS. *Blue Banner* [Onondaga Community College, Syracuse, N.Y.], 12 February 1971, p. 7.

Interview with Jerome Berrigan in which he speaks of his radical roots and his support of his brothers.

H-44 Melville, Marjorie and Thomas. THE CATHOLIC RESISTANCE [I and II]. New York *Times*, 26 April 1971, p. 22; 27 April 1971, p. 41.

A couple involved in the Catonsville 9 action discuss their act as one of loyalty to Christ and the United States.

H-45 Anderson, William R. IN DEFENSE OF THE FATHERS BERRI-GAN. *Catholic Mind* 69, May 1971, pp. 4-9.

A Tennessee Congressman defends Daniel and Philip Berrigan against charges lodged against them by then FBI director J. Edgar Hoover.

H-46 Day, Dorothy. THE BERRIGANS AND PROPERTY RIGHTS. Re-printed from the *Catholic Worker*. *Fellowship* 37, May 1971, p. 25.

The co-founder of the Catholic Worker movement pleads with Christian activists to follow the Golden Rule in their protest actions.

H-47 Jacobs, Jim. WITNESSES FOR PEACE? *Salt* [Syracuse, N.Y.] 1, 18 May 1971, pp. 16-18, 22-23.

A brief account of the development of the Berrigan witness.

H-48 Sandler, Corey. "A COMING TO AWARENESS." *Salt* [Syra-cuse, N.Y.] 1, 18 May 1971, pp. 19-21.

Jerome Berrigan talks about his parents and brothers and about Hoover's charges against the brothers for the kidnapping-bombing conspiracy.

H-49 Sisk, John P. CRISIS ON THE LEFT: THE BERRIGANS AND OTHER CATHOLIC INTRANSIGENTS. *Critic* 29, July-August 1971, pp. 18-26.

Finds the radical Left guilty of using the tactics of the radical Right in order to challenge the American system of politics.

H-50 Denman, Alvin L. SOME MEMOS ON "THE LAW" IN THE BERRI-
GAN CONSPIRACY CASE. *Lutheran Quarterly* 23, August
1971, pp. 231-239.

Notes on the components involved in the legal charges
lodged against the Harrisburg 8.

H-51 Zahn, Gordon. THE GREAT CATHOLIC UPHEAVAL. *Saturday
Review* 54, 11 September 1971, pp. 24-27, 54, 56.

Views the Berrigans as a small fringe (ultra resistance)
of the antiwar movement.

H-52 Wills, Garry. A REVOLUTION IN THE CHURCH. *Playboy* 18,
November 1971, pp. 159-160.

Discusses why Catholic FBI agents were pursuing Catholic radical priests Daniel and Philip Berrigan.

H-53 Bartelme, Elizabeth. VISITING DAN. *Critic* 30, November-
December 1971, pp. 66-68.

Sensitive personal account of visiting Daniel Berrigan
in Danbury Prison, written by his long-time editor and
friend.

1972

H-54 Bianchi, Eugene C. THE RELIGIOUS EXPERIENCE OF REVOLU-
TIONARIES. Garden City, N.Y.: Doubleday, 1972.

Contains a chapter on the revolutionary religion of
Daniel Berrigan.

H-55 Cargas, Harry J. DANIEL BERRIGAN AND CONTEMPORARY PRO-
TEST POETRY. New Haven: College University Press,
1972.

Contains one chapter on Daniel Berrigan, "THE POET AS
CITIZEN," in which Cargas notes the close relationship
between Daniel Berrigan's writing and life.

H-56 Day, Dorothy. ON PILGRIMAGE: THE SIXTIES. New York:
Curtis Books, 1972.

Selections from Dorothy Day's column "On Pilgrimage"
from the *Catholic Worker* during the 1960's. Contains
some observations on the Berrigans.

H-57 Douglass, James W. RESISTANCE AND CONTEMPLATION: THE
      WAY OF LIBERATION. Garden City, N.Y.: Doubleday, 1972.

      A theologian and friend of the Berrigans, who has pat-
      terned acts of resistance on the Baltimore and Catons-
      ville actions of the Berrigans, outlines a theology of
      resistance. Dedicated in part to Daniel and Philip
      Berrigan.

H-58 Halpert, Stephen, and Tom Murray (editors). WITNESS OF
      THE BERRIGANS. Garden City, N.Y.: Doubleday 1972.

      Contents:

      a Halpert, Stephen, and Tom Murray. PREFACE, pp. ix-
         xi.
      b Berrigan, Philip. PROLOGUE, p. xiii.
      c Zinn, Howard. THE PRISONERS: A BIT OF CONTEMPORARY
         HISTORY, pp. 3-18.
      d Cox, Harvey G., Jr. TONGUES OF FLAME: THE TRIAL OF
         THE CATONSVILLE NINE, pp. 19-23.
      e Mayer, Paul. A COURTROOM OUTSIDE THE WORLD: THE
         MILWAUKEE FOURTEEN VS THE STATE OF WISCONSIN,
         pp. 24-44.
      f AN INTERVIEW WITH ROBERT CUNNANE, pp. 45-62.
      g Finlay, Daniel. PERSONHOOD AND POETRY, pp. 65-83.
      h Forest, James H. DANIEL BERRIGAN: THE POET AND
         THE PROPHET AS PRIEST, pp. 84-110.
      i Coles, Robert. OUT OF STEP AND IN STEP, pp. 111-116.
      j Lockwood, Lee. BERRIGAN AT LARGE, pp. 117-139.
      k Berrigan, Daniel. SERMON FROM THE UNDERGROUND,
         2 August 1970, pp. 140-143.
      l Stringfellow, William. AN AUTHORITY OVER DEATH,
         pp. 146-154.
      m Callahan, Sidney Cornelia. THANK YOU, DAN, THANK
         YOU, PHIL, pp. 155-157.
      n Frain, William J. WHAT MAKES DANNY RUN, pp. 158-
         165.
      o Kunstler, William M. SOME THOUGHTS ABOUT THE BERRI-
         GANS, ET AL., pp. 166-172.
      p Dowd, Douglas. THE STRENGTHS AND LIMITATIONS OF RE-
         SISTANCE, pp. 175-188.
      q Davidon, Ann Morrissett. WAR RESISTANCE AND THE
         BERRIGANS, pp. 189-194.
      r A CONVERSATION WITH STAUGHTON LYND, pp. 195-198.
      s Berrigan, Daniel. EPILOGUE, pp. 199-200.

H-59   Nelson, Jack, and Ronald J. Ostrow. THE FBI AND THE
       BERRIGANS: THE MAKING OF A CONSPIRACY. New York:
       Coward, McCann, Geoghegan, 1972.

       Two reporters try to reconstruct events related to the
       government's conspiracy charges against Philip Berrigan
       and others.

H-60   O'Rourke, William. THE HARRISBURG 7 AND THE NEW
       CATHOLIC LEFT. New York: Thomas Y. Crowell, 1972.

       A novelist sketches his impressions of the Harrisburg
       trial. Contains lengthy quotations from the confiscated
       letters of Philip Berrigan and Elizabeth McAlister.

H-61   Wills, Garry. BARE RUINED CHOIRS. DOUBT, PROPHECY,
       AND RADICAL RELIGION. Garden City, N.Y.: Doubleday,
       1972.

       A lively and highly personal account of contemporary
       American Catholicism from Spellman to the Berrigans by
       a scholar and journalist.

H-62   Ludwig, Robert. IN SEARCH OF DANIEL BERRIGAN. *Listen-*
       ing 7, Fall 1972, pp. 140-161.

       The author's personal account of conversations with
       persons close to Daniel Berrigan.

H-63   Rasmussen, Larry. DANIEL BERRIGAN AND DIETRICH BON-
       HOEFFER: PARALLELS AND CONTRASTS IN RESISTANCE. *Dia-*
       logue 11, Autumn 1972, pp. 264-272.

       A comparison of Daniel Berrigan's and Dietrich Bon-
       hoeffer's thoughts on resistance, with special emphasis
       on their divergent attitudes on power and moral purity.

H-64   Neuhaus, Richard. THE GEOGRAPHY OF HEROISM. *Worldview*
       15, February 1972, pp. 9-19.

       An associate of Daniel Berrigan's from Clergy and Laity
       Concerned discusses the Christian implications of Ber-
       rigan's GEOGRAPHY OF FAITH.

H-65   Bach, John [Jon], and Mitchell Snyder. DANBURY: ANAT-
       OMY OF A PRISON STRIKE. *Liberation* 17, May 1972, pp.
       32-42.

       Two resisters, friends of the Berrigans, write of a
       prison strike at Danbury Federal Penitentiary.

H-66 Brown, Robert McAfee. REFLECTIONS ON DANIEL BERRIGAN. *Christian Century* 89, 17 May 1972, pp. 572-575.

Verse written after seeing picture of Daniel Berrigan's capture by FBI agents on Block Island in August 1970. Theme: "The cop is the captive and the prisoner is free."

H-67 Gray, Francine du Plessix. HARRISBURG: THE POLITICS OF SALVATION. *New York Review of Books*, 1 June 1972, pp. 34-40.

Part one of a dramatic and somewhat sensationalized account of the Harrisburg trial.

H-68 Gray, Francine du Plessix. THE POLITICS OF SALVATION II. *New York Review of Books*, 15 June 1972.

Concluding piece of a dramatic and somewhat sensationalized account of the Harrisburg trial.

H-69 Wills, Garry. LOVE ON TRIAL: THE BERRIGAN CASE RECONSIDERED. *Harper's* 245, July 1972, pp. 63-71.

Interpretation of Harrisburg trial as result of Berrigan circle's response to escalation of war with escalation of nonviolent activities.

H-70 Day, Dorothy. ON PILGRIMAGE. (Open letter to Daniel Berrigan). *Catholic Worker*, December 1972, pp. 2, 8.

In an open letter to Daniel Berrigan, Dorothy Day discusses her views on nonviolence and nonresistance.

H-71 Fager, Charles. SEARCHING, DAN BERRIGAN REVISITS SCRIPTURE. *National Catholic Reporter*, 22 December 1972, pp. 3, 6.

Daniel Berrigan discusses the Bible and the writings of Jacques Ellul.

1973

H-72 Coles, Robert. A SPECTACLE UNTO THE WORLD: THE CATHOLIC WORKER MOVEMENT. Photographs by Jon Erikson. New York: Viking Press, 1973.

Sympathetic account of the New York Catholic Worker.
Includes some photographs of Daniel Berrigan at the
New York Catholic Worker.

H-73   Weber, Paul J., S.J. DANIEL BERRIGAN: POLITICAL THEO-
       LOGY IN THE POST-WAR YEARS. *Chicago Studies* 12,
       Spring 1973, pp. 77-90.

       A political scientist presents several keys toward an
       understanding of Daniel Berrigan's political views.

H-74   Coleman, William E. RELIGION, PROTEST, AND RHETORIC.
       Foundations 16, January-March, 1973, pp. 41-56.

       Martin Luther King and Philip Berrigan are analyzed as
       prophets whose success in communicating their messages
       has made them unacceptable to many Americans.

H-75   Fager, Charles. RESISTANCE IN PRISON ON RISE---BERRI-
       GAN. *National Catholic Reporter*, 5 January 1973,
       pp. 1, 17.

       Philip Berrigan's views on the development of a resis-
       tance culture in prison.

H-76   Weber, Paul J., S.J. THEOLOGICAL RESISTANCE: MARTIN
       LUTHER KING AND DAN BERRIGAN. *Month* 6, February 1973,
       pp. 35-38, 45.

       Ways in which Martin Luther King, Jr., and Daniel Ber-
       rigan have broken with "classical" civil disobedience.

H-77   Forest, Jim [James H.]. HARRISBURG CONSPIRACY: THE
       BERRIGANS AND THE CATHOLIC LEFT. *WIN* 9, 15 March 1973,
       pp. 4-31.

       Forest, a close friend of the Berrigans, and a member
       of the Milwaukee 14, writes an intimate and sympathetic
       version of the Berrigans at the Harrisburg trial.

H-78   Ruether, Rosemary. MONKS AND MARXISTS: A LOOK AT THE
       CATHOLIC LEFT. *Christianity and Crisis* 33, 30 April
       1973, pp. 75-79.

       A theologian studies the American Catholic Left and its
       relation to Marxism. The Berrigans are viewed as mys-
       tics who wish to lead a supernatural transformation,
       not a political revolution.

H-79   Zinn, Howard. AMAZING GRACE: THE MOVEMENT WINS IN
       CAMDEN. *Liberation* 18, July-August 1973, pp. 4-5.

       A radical historian looks at the Camden 28 trial, at which
       Philip Berrigan testified on behalf of the defendants.

H-80 Berns, Walter. THE "ESSENTIAL SOUL" OF DAN BERRIGAN. *National Review* 25, 9 November 1973, pp. 1231-1234, 1239-1243.

A conservative political scientist expresses his differences with Daniel Berrigan's views on politics.

1974

H-81 Curtis, Richard. THE BERRIGAN BROTHERS: THE STORY OF DANIEL AND PHILIP BERRIGAN. New York: Hawthorn Books, 1974.

A simple descriptive account of the lives of Daniel and Philip Berrigan.

H-82 Raines, John C. (editor). CONSPIRACY: THE IMPLICATIONS OF THE HARRISBURG TRIAL FOR THE DEMOCRATIC TRADITION. New York: Harper and Row, 1974.

Contents:

a Brown, Robert McAfee. INTRODUCTION.
b Novak, Michael. "BLUE-BLEAK EMBERS...FALL, GALL THEMSELVES...GASH GOLD-VERMILLION."
c Waskow, Arthur I. AMERICAN CAPITALISM AND AMERICAN CATHOLICISM: ON COLLISION COURSE?
d Coles, Robert. ORDINARY HOPES, ORDINARY FEARS.
e Goldfarb, Ronald. POLITICS AT THE JUSTICE DEPARTMENT.
f Marshall, Burke. THE ISSUES ON TRIAL.
g Raines, John C. THE PURSUIT OF LEGITIMACY.

H-83 BERRIGAN TURNS DOWN PEACE PRIZE. *National Catholic Reporter*, 11 January 1974, pp. 3, 14.

Controversy over Daniel Berrigan's views on Israel lead him to reject the Gandhi Peace Award.

H-84 Cowan, Paul. THE MORAL IMPERIALISM OF DAN BERRIGAN. *Village Voice*, 31 January 1974, pp. 22-23.

Focusing on Daniel Berrigan's views on Israel, Paul Cowan concludes that Daniel Berrigan is no prophet, but a moral imperialist.

H-85 Chomsky, Noam. DANIEL IN THE LIONS' DEN: BERRIGAN & HIS CRITICS. *Liberation* 6, February 1974, pp. 15-24.

Part of a special issue of *Liberation* devoted to the questions raised by Daniel Berrigan on the Middle East.

H-86   Forest, Jim [James H.]. DANIEL BERRIGAN'S OUTRAGED LOVE. *Fellowship* 40, February 1974, pp. 2-3.

A personal friend defends Daniel Berrigan's views on Israel.

H-87   Ginsberg, Allen. JAWEH AND ALLAH BATTLE (for Dan Berrigan). *WIN* 10, 28 March 1974, pp. 12-13.

Poem commemorating Daniel Berrigan's receipt of War Resisters League award.

H-88   Jacobs, Paul. DANIEL BERRIGAN: SOME OF HIS BEST FRIENDS WERE.... *Ramparts* 12, April 1974, pp. 10-12.

Summarizes reactions of Daniel Berrigan's views on Israel and criticizes Berrigan's lack of knowledge on the issue while commending him for some of his views.

H-89   Novak, Michael. THE ORANGING OF THE BERRIGANS. *Christian Century* 91, 17 April 1974, pp. 417-422.

A Catholic scholar casts an unsympathetic glance at the Berrigans' politics.

H-90   McDougall, William Douglas. [CASE NOTES--U.S. V. BERRIGAN]. *Fordham Law Review* 42, May 1974, pp. 924-934.

Summary of legal issues involved in U.S. v. Berrigan, the case stemming from convictions against Philip Berrigan and Elizabeth McAlister for alleged letter smuggling.

H-91   Shapiro, Harriet. BERRIGAN IN CRISIS. *Intellectual Digest* 4, May 1974, p. 6+.

Harriet Shapiro interviews Daniel Berrigan on the question of Israel.

H-92   Mayer, Paul. PEACE, JUSTICE--AND THE PALESTINIANS. *WIN* 10, 4 July 1974, pp. 4-5.

A former Benedictine monk and friend, who accompanied Daniel Berrigan to the Middle East, writes on the political situation there.

H-93   Glick, Ted. AN OPEN LETTER OF RESIGNATION FROM THE CATHOLIC LEFT. *WIN* 10, 30 October 1974, pp. 17-18.

A critical response to Philip Berrigan's views as expressed in his article ON KINGMAKING.

H-94 Mayer, Paul. VOICES OF THE MIDDLE EAST. *WIN* 10,
5 December 1974, pp. 12-19.

Report by theologian and friend of Daniel Berrigan on
their trip to Middle East and their meetings with Pales-
tinian leaders.

1975

H-95 Patton, John H. RHETORIC AT CATONSVILLE: DANIEL BER-
RIGAN, CONSCIENCE, AND IMAGE ALTERATION. *Today's
Speech* 23, Winter 1975, pp. 3-12.

The Catonsville action is analyzed in rhetorical terms,
and the author concludes that conscience plays a major
role in joining words with deeds.

H-96 Cornell, Thomas. THE FIRST 10 YEARS OF THE CATHOLIC
PEACE FELLOWSHIP. *Catholic Peace Fellowship Bulletin*,
February 1975, pp. 5-6, 12-14.

One of the founders of the Catholic Peace Fellowship
talks about its roots, the Catholic Worker and Fellowship of Reconciliation, in particular.

H-97 Scott, L. PHIL BERRIGAN: NONVIOLENT RESISTANCE, SELF-
LIBERATION. Ithaca *New Times*, 9 February 1975, p. 4.

Contains Philip Berrigan's views on community and
revolution.

H-98 Vree, Dale. "STRIPPED CLEAN": THE BERRIGANS AND THE
POLITICS OF GUILT AND MARTYRDOM. *Ethics* 85, July 1975,
pp. 271-287.

Interprets the Berrigans' ideas on original sin as not
within the framework of traditional Christianity and
emphasizes "collective guilt" as a factor in their
politics.

1976

H-99   Deedy, John. THE CATHOLIC LEFT: AN ELEGY OF SORTS.
        Critic 34, Spring 1976, pp. 58-66.

        1975 Critic Lecture on the eclipse of the Catholic
        Left and the need for a more convincing witness.

H-100   True, Michael. POETRY AND THE VIETNAM VORTEX. *Cross
        Currents* 26, Summer 1976, pp. 251-256.

        Contains some astute comments on Daniel Berrigan's
        resistance poetry from his collection PRISON POEMS.

H-101   Sheats, Ladon. LADON SHEATS: PILGRIMAGE OF A PEACE-
        MAKER. INTERVIEW. *Sojourners* 5, March 1976, pp. 11-19.

        A member of Jonah House, Philip Berrigan's and Eliza-
        beth McAlister's resistance community, discusses their
        civil disobedience at the Pratt Whitney Aircraft plant.

H-102   Berrigan, Jerry [Jerome Charles]. POETRY AND POLITICS.
        Peace Newsletter [Syracuse Peace Council], August 1976,
        p. 11.

        Jerome Berrigan links politics, the art of the possible,
        to poetry writing.

H-103   Kiefer, Rita Brady. THE "FRAGILE UNKILLABLE FLOWER"
        OF DANIEL BERRIGAN'S POETRY. *Christian Century* 93,
        24 November 1976, pp. 1038-1042, 1047.

        A poet traces the growth and development of Daniel
        Berrigan's poetry.

1977

H-104   Maher, John. 90 PROTEST VIETNAM "REPRESSION."
        National Catholic Reporter, 7 January 1977, p. 16.

        Antiwar leaders, including the Berrigans, sign a letter
        protesting alleged repression on the part of the Viet-
        namese government.

H-105   Rashke, Richard. BERRIGANS BACK VIETNAM REGIME, CALL
        LETTER PUBLICITY "IRRESPONSIBLE." *National Catholic
        Reporter*, 14 January 1977, p. 3.

The Berrigans' response to publicity concerning a letter to the Vietnamese government on the human rights
issue.

H-106 Berrigan, Jerome Charles. JERRY BERRIGAN'S REFLEC-
TIONS FROM ALEXANDRIA JAIL. *Year One* [Baltimore], 3,
February 1977, p. 4.

A brother of Daniel and Philip Berrigan writes of his
jail sentence after he participated in a protest at
the Pentagon.

INDEXES

DANIEL BERRIGAN
Books and Articles

DANIEL BERRIGAN
Poetry by Title and First Line

A Brief Pause a Refreshment in the Course of, A-18-h
A Broadway hash joint, a Puerto Rican, A-13-aw, A-24-fr
A bronze head of Mallarmé by Picasso--, A-24-ea-5
A brutal landscape, A-7-az-12
A brutal landscape, they say, C-204
A cock mounted the tall, A-24-ab
a crowded car-load, A-22-t
A declarative. Man, A-5-ab
A doorway to seasons;, A-24-cs
A double heart be far from me, Lord, A-29-ah, C-524
A drain curved, A-13-bo
A fern at window, A-24-v
A flower is a single jeopardy--, A-13-i, A-24-el, C-341
a freak's eye, A-13-bp
a ghost in offstage darkness; no lines, A-5-q, A-24-bc
a lark must be, A-3-bd
A leaf's falling tells, A-5-m, C-134
A living eye rested on the book, A-7-b, C-166
A loaf of it shaped like God, A-13-bq
A magisterial touch was firm, A-5-ai, C-131
A maiden's untroubled speech, C-103
A man, a woman, their love, A-13-ay, A-24-ft, C-319
A mother blesses the Son, A-3-aa
A peace treaty signed, A-7-aq, C-163
A poor man's sleep (God says), C-258
A radiant trinity riding, A-7-v
A sick woman, C-365
A sidelong hairy look, A-13-ao, A-24-fk
A sword forbade me to grow old: it cut, A-3-n, C-89
A terror to the great one, A-29-v
A thousand-year-old corpse has no redress;, A-5-u, A-24-br
A wonder of origins; flower points to a bird, C-135
A year ago this autumn Tom Byers, A-22-bd
A young priest, dead suddenly, A-7-x, A-24-db
ABEL, A-3-b, A-24-r
ABELARD, C-6

about trees: past is never tall enough, A-3-ax, A-24-am
ABRAHAM, A-3-d, A-24-s, C-79
According to practically every Zen master who ever wrote,
  A-18-m
ACT OF LOVE, THE, A-7-t, A-24-cp
After moonrise tonight the snow lay, A-22-au
After my universe was only, A-5-y, C-71
After my world was only, A-24-cc
AGEMEMNON, A-13-bb
AIR MAIL LETTER, A-7-az-12, A-24-ea-12, C-204, C-207
AIR TRIP TO BOSTON, A-7-o, A-24-cm, C-177, C-181
Alas if a man's death, A-13-an, A-24-fj
ALERT, A-12-t, A-13-f, A-24-ei, C-336, C-342
ALL ALL COME BEFORE YOU / PSALM 81, A-29-y
All bets were on; he was dying, A-22-ab
[ALL CREATION], A-17-s
All creation, A-17-s
ALL DAY I CRY OUT TO YOU / PSALM 22, A-29-h
[ALL ELBOWS, CROOKS AND KNEES], A-16-j, A-17-t
All elbows, crooks and knees, A-16-j, A-17-t
All kinds of poets, believe me, could better praise your,
  A-20-y, A-24-gf-10
All night the fretful cricket, A-5-a, A-24-az
All their lives rounded in a backcountry brogue, A-1-d, C-39
All things despised, capricious, A-1-y
All things despised, capricious, cranky, A-24-j, C-520
Almighty God could make again, A-5-bg, A-24-bm, C-108
ALMOST EVERYBODY IS DYING HERE: ONLY A FEW ACTUALLY MAKE IT,
  A-22-i
always comes on strong, A-13-bx
AMBITION, C-486
AMERICA IS HARD TO FIND, A-20-b, C-404
American as the apple pie on your face, A-22-ax
[AMONG THE FLAG POLES], A-17-b
Among the flag poles, A-13-a-1, A-17-b, A-24-ec-1
An enormous encompassing weakness, A-22-bn
An old woman of hearth and field, A-5-bc, C-68
And, C-532
and a patchwork snow under inert trees:, A-1-v
AND HE FED THEM ALL, A-7-ad, A-24-df, C-193
and spoke: *coopers, craftsmen, shepherds*, A-5-bb, A-24-av,
  C-111
and the least of these, C-502
AND THE LORD ENTERS / PSALM 127, A-20-am
AND WHAT IS MAN, A-13-aw, A-24-fs, C-296
AND WHERE IN THE WORLD ARE YOU? / PSALM 73, A-29-t
And wonder why the cancer reconvenes, C-152
ANNOUNCEMENT, A-24-gf-1

It was in no sense shoring up the wall, C-327
It was November: an invisible fire, A-1-g, A-24-d
ITS PERFECT HEART, A-1-g, A-24-d

January; a sick woman, A-24-ge-3
Jesus came down from Crough Patrick, A-24-gd-5
Jesus says;, A-18-v
JEWEL, THE / (AT A LECTURE), A-7-bd
JOB, A-3-f
JOHN ANDERSON MY JO JOHN, A-13-at, A-24-fn, C-300, C-301
JOHN UREY, A-24-gb-3
JOSEPH, C-69, C-70
JOURNEY TO HANOI: A POETRY READING, C-342
JUBILEE, A-1-j
JUBILEE CHANT, C-21
JUBILEE CHANT (for Fathers Keyes and Brock), C-20
[JUDGE MACE HIS BLACK], A-17-f
Judge Mace his black, A-13-a-5, A-17-f, A-24-ec-5

KEEP THE HOUR, A-7-d, A-24-cg, C-225
KERMIT, A-22-h
Kildeers that once like leaves in autumn tempests, A-22-ao
KINDER TIMES?, A-5-be, A-24-au
KING CAME BEARING GIFTS, THE, A-7-g
know, A-13-y, A-24-ex

LABOR, THE, A-5-ab
LADEN FOG IT IS IN WELCOMING THIS UNIVERSAL ELEMENT WE STAND
  WITHIN REST WITHIN AND RISE EMBOLDENED BY THE TRUTH,
  A-18-i
Lady, the Maytime mirrors you very well--, C-1
LANDSCAPES THERE ARE, A-5-b, A-24-bn, C-51, C-138, C-139
Landscapes there are of such formal will and silken atmos-
  phere, C-138
LAST DAY, A-7-am, A-24-dy, C-168, C-172, C-376
LATE, A-3-bg
LAUREL, A-13-bk
LAZARUS, A-3-q, A-24-aa, C-69, C-71, C-102
LAZARUS / I, A-5-x, A-24-cb
LAZARUS / II, A-5-y, A-24-cc
Left New York by Mohawk jet, A-24-gc-1
LENS, THE, A-5-1, A-24-bo, C-133
LENT IS THE WORLD: LIFE, DEATH AND NEW LIFE ONCE MORE, C-237
LEPER, THE, A-7-j, A-24-co
let go days that are, A-3-u
Let there be man is one thing--but, A-24-cy
LET US MAKE TO OUR IMAGE, C-33
Let us pray; forgive the big ones Father, A-22-af

My cell gives on a barred window. At night, A-22-bm
[MY FACE WHITE AS A POWDERED CLOWN'S], A-26-v
My face white as a powdered clown's, A-26-v
MY FATHER, A-22-ab
My favorite lower case, A-24-gd-2
my 50th year having arrived, A-22-ae
My God, C-275
My grandmother, by time diminished, A-5-az, C-128
MY GUTS BEGIN, A-13-cc
My heart slows to my father's, A-3-e
MY HELP, MY HOPE / PSALM 121, A-29-ai, C-523, C-525
My laced and living memories arise, A-1-ad, C-36
MY LADY MARY, C-114
My little friend a flutist sits far side of the river,
  A-24-gf-7
MY LOVE SPOKE FOR ME (*for* Philip, on his profession), C-25
My mind had sought, C-17
MY MOTHER, A-5-ad, A-24-bx
MY NAME, A-12-y, A-13-1, A-24-eo
MY PLENTY, MY HARVEST / PSALM 53, A-29-o
My poor trees lean on sticks and complain, A-1-z
MYTHOLOGIES, A-24-cr

Nail him to sticks, A-3-au, A-24-ai, C-60
NAMELESS ODE, C-490
NATIVITY, C-142
Neither prideful nor superhuman--, A-24-bu
never a miracle!, A-13-bd
never eased life with miracles, C-318 .
NEWSSTAND, THE, A-7-az-9, A-24-ea-10, C-214
"NIGHT DARKENS THE SOUL OF MAN: BUT ONLY TO ILLUMINATE IT"
  WORDS ONCE MORE TAKEN FROM THE NOTES OF OUR GURU, A-18-aa
NIGHT FLIGHT TO HANOI, A-12-j, A-13-e, A-24-eh
Night to quiet countryside comes. The cathedral, A-3-bb
1969 OPENED LIKE THIS, A-24-ge-1, C-367, C-368
1961, A-5-af, A-24-bf
1967--VIETNAM, A-13-ag, A-24-fe
90 bawling years, then you died off, A-24-gd-6
NO AND YES AND THE WHOLE DAMN THING..., C-498, C-511
No Christ at a tombstone, A-3-r
No more austere, no more possessed he is, C-12
NO ONE KNOWS WHETHER DEATH, WHICH MEN IN THEIR FEAR CALL THE
  GREATEST EVIL, MAY NOT BE THE GREATEST GOOD, A-22-ai
No Swimming Aloud., A-17-k
no to you when we shut the front door and walk out and,
  A-23-f
No vine on the black hillside has death harvested, A-1-ah
NOE, A-3-c

Whenever I meet a crook, newly arrived, A-22-ar
Whenever I met a crook here, A-20-x, A-24-gf-9
Where great love is, A-24-ee
WHERE IN A SERIES OF CONTRADICTIONS IS POINTED OUT IN VIEW
  PERHAPS OF A RESOLUTION OF TRUTH, A-18-m
Where we have lighted, A-11-an
WHICH WAY IS MAN?, A-24-al
while yet this pitiful hour remains, we stand, C-8
Whispered to me: will you mount the waters?, A-3-c
WHO ARE WE, THAT YOU TAKE NOTE OF US? / PSALM 8, A-29-c
Who could declare your death, A-24-fu
Who could declare your death, standing, A-13-az, C-299
WHO ENTERS YOUR DWELLING, AN HONORED GUEST? / PSALM 15,
  A-29-f
Who loaded history's pig iron, A-13-am, A-24-fi, C-325
who without hands trouble the latch, A-24-bt
Who you are, A-1-aj, A-24-m-4
WHO'S WHO AT THE OBSEQUIES, A-24-ge-5, C-368, C-369
Why O God are you silent, A-29-u
will you for a space of days, A-11-ai, C-430
WINGS, A-24-gb-1
Winter is hard: it reminds us how that mother, C-31
Winter like a dust of snow, C-5
WINTER UPON OUR EYES, A-5-j, C-117
With a thoughtful spider to lace the window, C-9
With eyes a dying candle, A-1-e, C-15
[WITH REGARD TO THE GREAT YOU], A-30-d
with regard to the great You, A-30-d
With serious intent, He created, A-7-ba, C-202
Women who come to mummy you; trees, A-24-m-8
WONDER, A-24-dc
WONDER OF ORIGINS; A, A-5-n, C-135
Wonder why illness, A-7-y
Wood is noble when it forgets resemblance, A-24-ao
Wood is noble when it forgets to resemble, A-3-ap, C-97
Words are outer form, A-3-i, A-24-u
WORKMEN, THE, A-1-r, A-24-h, C-34
Wrapped like dead Jesus in 1) the American flag, A-13-br
WRITING OF A POEM, THE, A-7-c, A-24-cf, C-181, C-182

YEAR OF OUR LORD (Algeria, 1961), A-7-ai, A-24-dk, C-198
yesterday, the usual stiff-necked shakedown, A-22-m
YOU / PSALM 80, A-29-ab
You are condemned to the sleeplessness of god., C-485
You are not the golden Greek sea, no, A-7-az-3, A-24-ea-3
YOU COULD MAKE A SONG OF IT A DIRGE OF IT A HEARTBREAKER OF
  IT, A-22-o
YOU FINISH IT: I CAN'T, A-24-ch
you have surpassed your myths, A-13-bh

ADDRESS AT GETTYSBURG: CATHOLIC PRIEST SAYS VIETNAM WAR
DESTROYS HUMAN VALUES, F-27
AMERICAN KINGMAKING, D-5-c
AMERICA'S AFFAIR WITH THE BOMB, OR SPECULATIONS ON DEICIDE,
F-94
ANARCHY AND THE SUMMER CAMPAIGN, F-95
ANOTHER HELPER--ANOTHER BEAST, D-5-i, F-99
APOLOGIA FOR CAT, AN, F-55
ARNOLD'S VICTORY, D-5-d, F-79
[AUTHOR'S NOTE], D-3-c

BALTIMORE, MARYLAND / APRIL 1973, D-4-i
BERRIGAN CASE, THE, (EXCERPT FROM STATEMENT PRIOR TO COURT
SENTENCE), F-46
BLACK MAN'S BURDEN, F-22
BLOOD, WAR AND WITNESS, E-2

CAN WE SERVE BOTH LOVE AND WAR?, D-3-d
CATHOLIC CHURCH AND THE NEGRO, F-11
CATONSVILLE NINE: STATEMENTS AT SENTENCING, C-363
CHALLENGE OF SEGREGATION, THE, F-2, F-3
CHRIST AND THE SHAPE OF MANKIND, D-1-c, F-10
CHRISTIAN WITNESS TODAY, F-17
CHRISTIANITY IN HARLEM, F-19
CHRONICLE OF HOPE, A, [:] THE JONAH HOUSE OF RESISTANCE [,]
1973-1977, D-5-1
CHURCH AND THE WORLD, THE, D-1-h
CLARIFICATION OF REVOLUTION, BERRIGAN STYLE, F-59
COLD-WAR ASPIRATIONS AND SECRETS, D-2-e
COLLAPSE OF AMERICA'S INDOCHINA EMPIRE, THE, F-85
COLOR OF POVERTY, THE, D-2-b
COMMUNITY IN THE MIDST OF VIOLENCE, F-86
COMMUNITY OF NINE, A, D-3-g
CONCERNING THANKSGIVING--AMERIKAN OR REAL?, F-96
CONSENSUS SOCIETY! CONSENSUS CHURCH?, D-2-a
CONVERSATIONS ON REVOLUTION, F-39, F-40, F-41, F-43

ELIZABETH McALISTER BERRIGAN
Works

ASKING CARTER TO TAKE HIS FAITH SERIOUSLY, G-18

CONTEMPLATIVE ACTION, G-12

FEMINISTS FOR LIFE, G-7
FORMING COMMUNITY: BALTIMORE'S JONAH HOUSE, G-5

INEVITABLE DESTRUCTION OR NEW POSSIBILITIES, G-13
INTERVIEW WITH LIZ McALLISTER [sic], PHIL BERRIGAN, DAN BER-
RIGAN, AN, G-15

LETTERS FROM BERRIGAN CASE, G-2
LIZ McALISTER'S STATEMENT PRIOR TO RESENTENCING--JANUARY 24,
1977, G-14

[MESSAGE FROM JAIL IN ALEXANDRIA, VIRGINIA], G-16

PRICE OF MAKING PEACE, THE, G-10
PRISON LETTER: RAISING CHILDREN, RESISTANCE, COMMUNITY, A,
G-17
PROPOSAL FOR A NATIONAL DEBATE ON NUCLEAR POLICY, G-11

REVIEW OF *CONSPIRACY: THE IMPLICATIONS OF THE HARRISBURG
TRIAL*, G-8

SISTER ELIZABETH McALISTER: AN INTERVIEW, G-1
SOIL FOR SOCIAL CHANGE, G-4
SOME REFLECTIONS ON THE MEANING OF RESISTANCE, G-6

TEXT OF THE BERRIGAN-McALISTER STATEMENT, G-3

VIETNAM: A CASE FOR REMEMBERING, G-9

SECONDARY SOURCES
Authors

Anderson, William R., H-33, H-45

Bach, John, D-5a, H-65
Bartelme, Elizabeth, H-53
Berns, Walter, H-80
Berrigan, Jerome C., A-20-a, H-4, H-102, H-106
Bianchi, Eugene C., H-54
Bienek, Horst, B-16
Boyd, Malcolm, B-4
Brown, Robert McAfee, H-41-g, H-66, H-82-a

Callahan, Sidney Cornelia, H-58-m
Cameron, J.M., H-7
Cargas, Harry James, H-18, H-55
Casey, William Van Etten, B-12, H-41, H-41a
Chomsky, Noam, H-41-e, H-85
Clifford, Richard J., H-41-c
Coffey, Thomas, H-1
Coleman, William E., H-74
Coles, Robert, A-19, A-19-a, H-41-xe, H-58-i, H-72, H-82-d
Committee on New Alternatives in the Middle East, B-26, B-27
Cornell, Thomas Charles, H-13, H-96
Cowan, Paul, H-41-xc, H-84
Cox, Harvey G., Jr., H-58-d

Cunnane, Robert, H-58-f
Curtis, Richard, H-81

Davidon, Ann Morrissett, H-58-q
Day, Dorothy, B-14, H-32, H-46, H-56, H-70
Deedy, John, H-99
De Leon, Shirley, H-2
Deming, Barbara, H-17
Denman, Alvin L., H-50
Douglass, James W., H-10, H-57
Dowd, Douglas, H-58-p
Duff, Edward, H-41-b

Fager, Charles, H-71, H-75
Federal Bureau of Investigation, H-41-k
Ferber, Michael, H-34
Finlay, Daniel, H-58-g
Finn, James, B-3, E-1, H-8
Fitch, Robert Beck, B-10, H-24, H-30, H-35
Forest, James H., H-41-xb, H-58-h, H-77, H-86
Four Families, H-41-xd
Frain, William J., H-58-n

Ginsberg, Allen, H-87
Glick, Ted, H-93
Goldfarb, Ronald, H-82-e
Gray, Francine du Plessix, H-21, H-22, H-23, H-28, H-41-i, H-67, H-68

SECONDARY SOURCES
Titles

ABSURD CONVICTIONS, MODEST HOPES, A-21
AFTERWORD BY THICH NHAT HANH, A-29-as
AMAZING GRACE: THE MOVEMENT WINS IN CAMDEN, H-79
AMERICAN CAPITALISM AND AMERICAN CATHOLICISM: ON COLLISION
   COURSE?, H-82-c
AMERICAN CATHOLIC EXODUS, E-2
ARTIST AS PROPHETIC ACTIVIST, THE, H-19
AUTHORITY OVER DEATH, AN, H-58-1

BARE RUINED CHOIRS, H-61
BERRIGAN: A PHOTO ESSAY, H-30
BERRIGAN AT LARGE, H-58-j
BERRIGAN BROTHERS: THE STORY OF DANIEL AND PHILIP BERRIGAN,
   THE, H-81
BERRIGAN IN CRISIS, H-91
BERRIGAN IN HIS POEMS, H-12
BERRIGAN TURNS DOWN PEACE PRIZE, H-83
BERRIGANS, THE, B-12, H-41-x
BERRIGANS AND AMERICA, THE, H-41-h
BERRIGANS AND PROPERTY RIGHTS, THE, H-46
BERRIGANS BACK VIETNAM REGIME, CALL LETTER PUBLICITY "IRRE-
   SPONSIBLE," H-105
BERRIGANS: CONSPIRACY AND CONSCIENCE, THE, H-42
BERRIGANS--FRENETIC, THE, H-41-d
BERRIGANS--PROPHETIC?, THE, H-41-c
BERRIGANS: SIGNS OR MODELS?, THE, H-41-g
BEYOND CONFRONTATION: THE THERAPEUTIC TASK, H-41-xa
"BLUE-BLEAK EMBERS...FALL, GALL THEMSELVES...GASH GOLD-
   VERMILLION," H-82-b
BUDDHISTS IN VIETNAM, THE, B-25
BURDEN OF THE BERRIGANS, THE, H-41, H-41-b

[CASE NOTES--U.S. V. BERRIGAN], H-90
CATHOLIC LEFT: AN ELEGY OF SORTS, THE, H-99

RHETORIC AT CATONSVILLE: DANIEL BERRIGAN, CONSCIENCE, AND
   IMAGE ALTERATION, H-95
RUETHER'S OPEN LETTER TO DANIEL BERRIGAN, H-14

SEARCHING, DAN BERRIGAN REVISITS SCRIPTURE, H-71
SEEDS OF LIBERATION, B-19, B-20, B-21, B-23, B-24
SENATOR GOODELL & PHILIP BERRIGAN: AN UNTOLD STORY, H-31
"SILENCED" PRIESTS--A SPECIAL ISSUE, THE, H-6
SOAP BOX [EDITORIAL], H-20
SOME MEMOS ON "THE LAW" IN THE BERRIGAN CONSPIRACY CASE, H-50
SOME THOUGHTS ABOUT THE BERRIGANS, ET AL., H-58-o
SPECTACLE UNTO THE WORLD: THE CATHOLIC WORKER MOVEMENT, A,
   H-72
SPIRIT OF MODERN SACRED ART, THE, B-1
STRENGTHS AND LIMITATIONS OF RESISTANCE, THE, H-58-p
"STRIPPED CLEAN:" THE BERRIGANS AND THE POLITICS OF GUILT AND
   MARTYRDOM, H-98
SUSPECT TENDERNESS: THE ETHICS OF THE BERRIGAN WITNESS, B-13,
   H-39
SYRACUSE TO MONTGOMERY--AND BACK, H-4

TACTICS FAIL THE VISION, H-15
THANK YOU, DAN, THANK YOU, PHIL, H-58-m
THEOLOGICAL RESISTANCE: MARTIN LUTHER KING AND DAN BERRIGAN,
   H-76
THEOLOGY OF DANIEL BERRIGAN, THE, H-40
THINKING ABOUT THOSE PRIESTS, H-41-xe
TONGUES OF FLAME: THE TRIAL OF THE CATONSVILLE NINE, H-58-d
TRIAL BY AUTOPSY (CATONSVILLE 9 VS. JUDGE THOMSEN), H-17

ULTRA-RESISTANCE, THE, H-21
UNDERGROUND CHURCH, THE, B-4

VANISHING SPECIES, B-28
VISITING DAN, H-53
VOICES OF THE MIDDLE EAST, H-94

WAR RESISTANCE AND THE BERRIGANS, H-58-q
WHAT IS A CHRISTIAN?, H-7
WHAT MAKES DANNY RUN, H-58-n
WHOSE HEAVEN, WHOSE EARTH?, H-37
WITNESS OF THE BERRIGANS, B-15, B-17, E-3, H-58
WITNESSES FOR PEACE?, H-47